IF YOU'RE MY SOUL-MATE, WHY ARE YOU...

RUNNING

AWAY ?!

(confessions of a "developing" mystic)

by

JAY

A Children's Story for <u>Adults</u> About "Real" Relationships

©1991, JAY

Published by: Inspiration House
Vero Beach, Florida

Front cover
illustration: Anne Kerr

Printed by: R. R. Donnelley & Sons Company
Crawfordsville, Indiana

ISBN: 0-910668-06-X

4/92

Library of Congress Cataloging in Publication Data

Jay, 1944-
    If you're my soul-mate, why are you--running away?! :
(confessions of a "developing" mystic) / by Jay.
        p.   cm.
    "A children's story for adults about 'real' relationships."
    ISBN 0-910668-06-X
    1. Spiritual life. 2. Interpersonal relations.
I. Title. II. Title: Running Away?!.
BL624.J444 1991
131--dc20

Running Away

Why is it
that after you
have run away
I find myself
turning around
and walking back
to you ?
Could it be
that I always
hear your heart
calling for Love ?

Contents

AUTHOR'S NOTE

The most difficult time I have ever had on this earth is in my one-on-one boy-girl relationships...some times to the point where I became physically incapacitated because I took my physical separation from the woman in my life *so seriously.* You'd think that a person on his way to becoming a mystic would not fall into the "neediness" trap that other earthlings do. Well...*everyone* on Earth suffers to some degree because they "believe" that they are a *human* being (rather than a *spiritual* being, first and foremost) regardless of how "advanced" they are! We are *all* here to work out our *un*forgiveness of "ourselves" as demonstrated by the faults that we see in our closest companions. And, remembering the concept that "it takes one to know one," I decided it was time that I explore *my* deficiencies and fears exhibited by five, very significant *spiritual partners* (soul-mates) that I had over a ten year period...particularly, when the fifth one (who told me that she was a female version of me) left!

So, come on along as I share this tale with you about the Puppy Dog Man and the Cat Women...a man who would not *willingly* go away no matter how afraid his female partners were of total commitment to a whole and open relationship. (Maybe you will see yourself in these pages?!) Since we *all* act like children in this world (from an a-cosmic consciousness standpoint), this is a children's story for *adults* about "real" relationships as we continue to really grow-up when we look closely at ourselves through the *mirror* known as a soul-mate.

other books by JAY

BANISHED... From the Sandbox

To
Suzanne,
Roseanne,
Sandy,
Connie,
Robilee,
Josephine,
Gracie,
Bobbie,
Bobby,
Erika,
and...Eden

Me and Ralph

With clenched teeth and clenched fists at my side as I stood up, I yelled, "God...if I meet *another* woman who wants to learn the Truth or find her soul-mate in me or become my spiritual partner, I'll tell her to go shit in her hat!" (And, I did a week later.)

"Hold on, Jay!" said Ralph with great concern as he stood eye ball to eye ball with me now and put his hands on my shoulders and guided me backwards and sat me down on the porch swing. He had never seen me *openly* angry before (*very* few people ever have. My *own* anger scares me so much that I decided when I was 24 and knocked a whole bunch of cologne bottles off a dresser in a fit of anger directed at my first wife, who was frequently emotionally-explosive, that I *never* wanted to express anger violently again...verbally or physically. It's "rarely" part of my human nature.) Ralph stretched out on the rope hammock to my left. "God's not in the dream-world. He could care less about your *self-created* human problems."

I started again, less vehemently this time. "Suzanne talked to me much more openly two years *after* we were divorced than the guy she married after me. Roseanne told me *after* she left me that her time with me was the happiest in her life; yet, when the *realness* of my love for her was "psychically" brought to her attention, she ignored it. Connie thought I was the most mellow, spiritual man *sent* to her (psychically) at *her* request; yet never came back. Robilee heard *numerous* psychic clues as to our joined minds (in Spirit) and still ran away. Josephine ignored three *very obvious* "psychic" demonstrations of our spiritual bond, not to mention her own *deep* feelings of love for me, to fall back into the sandbox (called Earth-life) like a child.

"Ralph?"

"Yes, Jay."

"I can't figure it out!" I hesitated feeling frustrated.

"What?" he said lazily, lying in the hammock with his eyes closed.

I was gliding back and forth slowly on the hanging swing next to him on the back porch and staring blankly out over sparse, scrub oak bushes and tall, oriental-looking cedar trees gracing the grass-strewn sandy hill that sloped down toward the ocean. The sun had just set and the air was very still. You could almost hear your heart beating. I was pondering a long-time dilemma that had been plaguing me for several years...because I never understood (forgetting that "[intellectual] *understanding* is the booby-prize") how or why *they* left me, particularly since there was no fight or argument before they walked away. (When I went after them shortly after they departed our special-love relationship, they avoided me like a bad disease, which always surprised me since I had always been kind, loving, peaceful and allowed them to do pretty much what *they* wanted.)

"What is it?" Ralph said again, realizing that I was deeply saddened by *my* thoughts, as true friends whose minds are joined pick up.

With much surrender in my voice, speaking softly and slowly, I said, "I can't understand why over the past 10 years I have had *five* (female) spiritual partners, or *soul-mates* as a lot of people like to call them; and each of them has run away (figuratively) and walked back into the world and became a part 'of' it again. (Sorry...it is only a myth that we have just *one*!)

"I can't tell you how frustrating and humbling it is when your 'spiritual' partner walks away for no *sane* reason, even in Earth-terms. It's like being the most helpless you've ever been short of dying. Thoughts like 'Father, what have I done to deserve this?' *hammer* at you...over and over...in your mind, particularly when you've been devoting your life to learning and walking the spiritual (mystical) path to the full realization of God/ Love (*what* we join with when we surrender our ego...our *belief* in our sole existence as 'human' beings) as I have during this period. And, there's *no* logical reason like a big fight, fault-finding or incompatible life-styles to cause the parting.

"I watched five soul-mates run away and was not able to retrieve any of those relationships no matter what

I said to them afterwards. Five potentially near-perfect relationships turned to dust! If I did not have to stay in the physical universe after their departure, I wouldn't have minded I suppose...but, to hang out in the 'dream-world' without someone to talk with, in addition to our *real* Self, and share with gets pretty lonely and boring.

"You're a great friend, Ralph, and a good sounding board to explore and learn from my *own* thoughts...but, it would have been nice to have had one of them stay to *finish* walking all the way with me until my, and hopefully their, end of time on Earth. I just wanted a dedicated, female spiritual partner who knew THE Truth (that God did not make the physical universe and that this world is nothing more than a 'waking dream') and wanted to demonstrate, with me, how to live that life while here. Let's face it, Ralph, you're not my type to sleep and confer with in the middle of the night if I needed to share with someone then. Plus, women are the only kind of social and sexual companions I like.

"Accepting the Truth, I feel 'whole' (what 'holy' really means) and complete for the *most part*. But something, keeps gnawing at me that says, 'It sure would be *nice* to have a constant female spiritual companion to walk Home with.' I've had a beautiful *glimpse* of it five times. It's just tough *some* times still 'feeling' like a human being with all its needs and frailties, when I know better and can usually discipline and counsel my self through my own spiritual (Christ) consciousness by surrendering my focus and belief in my humanness. Human existence is not an easy *habit* to get over."

"Well, having gone through that kind of experience,

too, I can relate to the feelings of emptiness and the 'lack of control' you have, and I had, in those situations," said Ralph slowly and calmly.

"I guess I am hoping that my last spiritual partner, Josephine (Jo), who decided six months ago that she didn't want to continue our relationship without any warning that something was wrong or that she was unhappy with me, will wake-up and realize what we *really* have going for us. If she and the others were *just* 'spiritual plebeians,' to quote Jo, I could easily understand our parting since I tend to be pretty singular in my life purpose of *bringing Love* to others by living a quiet, but not inactive, life with a peaceful attitude devoid of all *value* judging...offering to assist anyone as a friend and brother to understand their spiritual reality as Mind (Spirit) that does not depend on its identity with the physical body even though they *choose* that existence to be here on Earth.

"To me, once you understand and experience this Truth, and Jo definitely had for instance, you don't (have to) walk back into the world and become part 'of' it (mentally), again! That's like *deliberately* forgetting everything you came here to understand and feel *in your heart*. Because *I* can't do that, I don't understand how others do...particularly, my past five spiritual partners.

"I think I need to 'explore' this dilemma of mine, that I accept that *I* have created, because I have learned that *everything* that happens to us on Earth is *our* wish since we write our own 'life scripts.' So, if you don't mind, Ralph, I would like to really discover, in depth, how and why I've setup these situations with these beautiful people. I want to get to the bottom of this, once and for all. Every situation and relationship in my life has been cleared *after* acknowledgment by forgiving myself 'in' them (realizing that they are mirrors of *my* past). Everyone really only talks to *themself*, although it seems otherwise, because *no one* can understand the 'meaning' of our thoughts and feelings but ourself."

"Sure...go ahead, I don't mind," yawned Ralph.

       *   *   *

I always kind of admired Ralph...or I should say my *ego* did...because he had courage to speak and live his life as he saw it. I had always been cautious until I noticed these traits in him. He was kind of an alter-ego for me... a true friend that I could always respect and trust... because I could overlook (forgive), particularly in the last few years, all his ego traits (and mine, since "it takes one to know one") and see his *innocence*.

When I first became aware of Ralph's presence in my life as a *mirror* into which I could look to heal many unforgivenesses in myself was eight years ago in Salt Lake City, Utah. We were close the first couple of years then as I *scrutinized* everything about him as a learning vehicle to overcome my unhealed opinions about my self. Then, I lost contact with him for the next six years as I went on my own deep spiritual quest for my *True Self* in southern Florida, where I have been living ever since. Recently, he has come back into my life; this time as a different kind of person...but then, so am I. And "like does attract like" as my friend, Richard, discovered.

When I first got to know Ralph, he had just come down off of a long journey of searching for fame, fortune, power and physical pleasure in the world in "human" terms (superficial, surface-striving for materialistic and intellectual achievement) and was "burned-out." Every negative quality I had ever had he manifested...sometimes by showing me the *opposite* quality such as he was very brave and confident with women, where I was not, to the point where he dated three to four different women during the week and took his weekends off to rest and play by himself. He had a *lot* of professional jobs in a relatively short period of time, where I prefer to have a singular direction, to the point that he would have been considered a chronic "job-hopper." If he didn't like something, whether it was a job or a woman, he left. He had no sense of commitment, which I think started when his efforts to maintain his relationship with his daughters from his previous marriage were severely hampered by their mother. I think he just found that he couldn't *control* the world, so he went in search of happiness in *things* like jobs, money, homes and women.

Recently, like me, he discovered our higher meaning in life as *spiritual beings* having a *human experience* here in the physical universe. Ralph learned that we *all* are playing "roles" for each other based upon *our* mutual, unconscious pact (what I call the "silent contract"), which may not be "knowable" to us here as we walk through life. So, he has learned to take life easy, as it comes, without any *predetermined* decisions as to what he should do or be beyond *this* moment. (In my case, I write books as they come.) To most earthlings, he would be categorized as a "free spirit," which unbeknownst to many is what we *all* are!

A short while back, I began experiencing terrible depression (self-hatred) over my long history of low self-esteem because of never being "supported" in my *entire* life to be or do any thing until I was 41 when my parents told me (when it no longer mattered) that they thought that I had more "raw talent" than anybody they knew. (Their comment was very appreciated though!) I, of course, started listening to my *ego*, which stays *in control* by either keeping me occupied and busy in worldly activities or fault-finding of my human qualities, and began having suicide thoughts. Well, Ralph and I went for a walk together on the beach near my home. He talked and I listened. Ralph reminded me that my "ego" was just my *false* belief in my self as *only* a human being and that *it* would always put me down and try to kill me eventually when I realized that I could *never* "control" the world to have things my way. He reiterated that I am "Spirit" in reality and that I was too smart now to let a *belief system* (which is all the ego is) over-power me. Silently, I agreed, and an hour later I was okay...my mind was healed again.

Here this *essence*, which I used to criticize and evaluate years ago, had grown into this lovely spiritual entity that was acting like my guardian angel now, helping me to get through *one* of those periods in my life that are frequently called "dark nights of the soul." Amazing how things flip-flop and change for the better when we let go of *value* judging and our opinions! Here

Ralph is once again, assisting me to understand one of my longest and most perplexing Earth-life experiences. What a blessing! I am very thankful to have him, as well as everyone, in my life.

★   ★   ★

"I have the next two weeks free to spend with you here in your lovely home. So, I'll just kick-back, relax and enjoy the peacefulness and quietness of *your* environment," said Ralph. "You're a gracious host, Jay, and it's always nice to be with you. We haven't spent a considerable amount of time together in the last six years, so this will be nice to *share* with you again...and you're a very giving/sharing person, which makes it very worthwhile and heart-warming for me, too, since you're so open. It will be fun to go 'mind-exploring,' which is *truly* the only kind there is, with you again. You are my best friend on Earth, and you helped keep me 'in-line' seven years ago. So...I will enjoy returning the favor. Why don't you begin with your first *known* spiritual partner, Suzanne?" Ralph counseled me as he lay there in the hammock with his eyes wide-open now expressing a deep, loving concern and an ability to listen *intently* (that I had *only* experienced with Jo before).

It takes a certain "gentleness" that's not of this Earth to convey that type of sincerity in such a loving and kind way. I felt truly honored to be in his presence, which is very Christ-like now.

It had gotten dark as I gently swung back and forth

at a pace that felt very soothing. The night air was balmy and a comfortable 77°F. (It's usually like summer in this part of Florida because the Gulf Stream comes within three miles of the eastern coastline.) Here were two grown men in their mid-forties having maintained their youthfulness, through no effort of their own (which was an example of that ageless-quality that seekers of the *true* mystical way of living in the physical realm typically project because of their inner-belief in the innocence of everyone and the understanding of *absolute* Truth), *joined* in peacefulness like two probing "wisemen" in their *singular* effort to discover and get beyond the most significant learning lesson...relationships!

Looking upward, with my eyes closed, I reflected back to 10 years ago when I met Suzanne....

The Mirror Remembered

I looked
into the mirror
and the mirror
looked back at me
as if to say,
"Do you see me
as you are,
because I am
your inside
on the outside ?!"

Suzanne
(Fairy-Tale Princess)

It was a cool (35°F), dry, clear and sunny day in Salt Lake City, Utah in January 1979 when I strolled into a computer manufacturer's headquarters all dressed-up in my finest blue checked suit for an interview with the head of marketing about a career-type position. After I introduced myself to the receptionist, I sat down on the sofa in the lobby and waited until this tall (5'9"), slender, very attractive, sultry-looking, sophisticated young lady with a peaches and cream complexion, light blue eyes and short, champagne-blond hair dressed in a rust colored pant-suit came up to me.

"Hello, my name is Suzanne. Don will see you now. Will you follow me?" as she lead me through the maze of desks and open-partitioned offices.

We hardly said much then as I was focused on meeting Don and gearing myself up for the interview. After it was through, about an hour later, I walked out of his office to Suzanne, whose desk was positioned across from Don's doorway, and commented on her perfume. She recoiled shyly with a beautiful "innocent" smile that captivated my heart immediately. I asked her for a date, and she blushingly agreed. (Since I had the old salesman's "killer instincts" in those days, I thought smugly to myself, "If Don doesn't give me a position, I'll at least have his secretary. A salesman always trys to 'close' [win] *something* during a call." I was one super-ego then, who *trained* himself from being a fearful, quiet, unassuming young man to be a "controller.")

Well, on our first date, Suzanne and I went snow skiing in Park City with a male friend of mine. I acted like a horse's ass by the end of the day (I got totally arrogant and ego-centered), and she would not have anything to do with me until I *profusely* apologized two weeks later.

Over the next three years, we lived together and moved apart goodly distances three times. We became *trusted* friends of each other's deepest, darkest secrets. Although I didn't have any, I *dragged* hers out of her over a three month period. She had *tremendous* guilt because of two affairs she had had. She became convinced that she was "okay" because she couldn't believe that some-one like me would love her unconditionally in spite of her immoral past (according to Suzanne). She once acknowledged that she was a "raunchy puritan" (as was I).

Suzanne thanked me two years after our physical relationship ended for *always* loving her ("I always knew that you loved me," she said) and for being the *only* person she could *always* turn to (more so than any of her family or friends) when she was in need of a *real* friend. She brought me a plaque and card that "thanked me for everything" (the sign that a relationship is *healed*, and therefore, physically over). She even called me on her wedding day to thank me "for being a very special part of [her] life." It was nice to be a *real* friend and confidant (my first time), and I told her that *her* happiness was my greatest pleasure and wished her well in her new and hopefully long-lasting relationship. (This was *the* way to end a relationship positively!)

Suzanne (she never liked to be called "Suzy" or any other nickname) and I had shared a lot together: we were both in the professional business world, were impeccable dressers, skied, shared all of our most lurid sexual fantasies, rode horses, went for late night drives in the car, danced a lot and shopped. I "adored" just *being* with her. She was a handsome, classy woman and my fairy-tale princess (you know...the one you always dream about finding). I even married her on Valentine's Day in 1982 only to have the marriage end in annulment two months and three days later because she panicked when I lost my job and she needed the formal approval of her brother and two sisters of our relationship, which never came.

*   *   *

Suzanne held up the mirror of *my* greatest fear at that time (but, I didn't realize it then) which was "financial insecurity." The women in my family were obsessed with money as indicated by their constant focusing on accumulating it and what things cost. Saving money (like in discount shopping) was the thing they did *best* and the *only* way they could *ensure* themselves of having some "control" in the world. Actually, this fear covered over my deep inner desire "to be taken care of" which I did not discover until three years later when I moved to Florida.

Also, the mere fact that we kept coming together and moving apart physically pointed out her fear of making a 100% commitment to our relationship since *she* kept leaving me. Yet, this is the woman that acknowledged to me, "You're what I've *always* wanted" (and, she for me), which no one has ever said before or since. Even though we *both* agreed to our annulment (I told her after I lost my job just weeks after our marriage that if *she* couldn't mentally and emotionally support me and us no matter what, *we* had no business being married), I realized later that she was *just fearful* and had I not been preoccupied with *my* plight and my *repressed* anger at her running away I could have stayed my ground and refused to throw in the towel on our marriage.

Two years later, I discovered that we were still friends as we sat in her car and smoked cigarettes (a new habit for her) and talked like old cronies for two hours while her boy-friend stayed in their apartment and watched football on the TV. Suzanne then confided in me that she *hated* "to lose control" of anything in her life. I never heard anyonelse (to this day) make that honest an admission. (After the first three months of our relationship, Suzanne was always the *most open* person in describing her "feelings." I have not seen anyone who could do so since.) Of course, this is THE *big* fear for all of us. No one is *willing* to totally surrender being "in control" of their life.

Now, one of the qualities of a close, intimate, special-love relationship (although many may not think of it in a positive way) is the *opportunity to expose* all of *your* insecurities and anxieties, which for most people lie buried deep as unrecognized guilt and experienced in the physical world as "fear." For instance, Suzanne's mood would change sometimes every couple of hours, which I *chose* to feel very insecure about because "I" could not control it. For the most part, I kept my peace, which is all anyone can do in those situations, and did not respond emotionally to her. (Since I had mood changes, I could notice them in her.)

She was probably one of the most noticeably "self-concerned" people I've ever known. Suzanne used to cry when she felt that *her* life-style would decline in any way. Her father even told her to "loosen-up" shortly after we were married. But, of course, everyone who comes to Earth does so to have their *own* way *first* and to be *special*, which includes me. (God would *not* make us "special." That's why we made up this "dream-world" we live in, so that we could *play* at becoming unique, better and having more than each other.)

To illustrate the severity to which her (and my) ego's

self-concern got, there was a time I ended up in the hospital to have lower-back surgery for a nerve condition, which caused me to fall down, that was a symptom of the *insecurity* I felt in our relationship. (All physical ailments are caused by our mind.) After the operation, which had a long, painful recuperation period, and while I was still in the hospital, Suzanne walked into my room one night, *announced* that "we never had a happy relationship" and turned around and left. *I* went after her some two weeks later when I got out of the hospital and could barely walk. (I kept going after her because I could feel her heart, as my *own*, "calling for love," which is what we are all doing when we are not giving it. People who *desperately need* love will run away from it because they feel unworthy and don't trust, or believe in, their *own* ability to love, so how can they trust anyonelse?! Also, their neediness will take the form of increased sexuality, which has nothing to do with love.)

(NOTE: The day before when I wrote the above paragraph I put an "X" through it after I finished it because my *ego* thought that it wasn't necessary to drag up this unpleasant part of my past. "It" never wants us to acknowledge what *it* made. *Today*, the "X" was gone!)

     ★   ★   ★

Because of Suzanne's child-like preoccupation with herself *first* (although she was also one of the *most* thoughtful and generous people I've ever known), I suffered from "uncertainty" frequently (which was *my* choice). I never knew if I could count on her to be there for me. Consequently, although I was *her* truest friend on Earth, I didn't feel like she was *mine*...very unfortunately. (Much later, I learned that our real, higher Self is the *only* one I, and we, can *ever* truly count on!)

⋆   ⋆   ⋆

Looking back over our years together, I felt like I gave her "freedom" (the only *true* gift of Love) to expose all her fears and experience all her sexual desires to the point of taking her from no orgasms (which are nothing more than physical expressions of our ability to spiritually "release/surrender" our control of the world through our bodies) to two a night. I also got to experience *my* devotion and "unconditional love" for Suzanne by assisting her to uncover her deepest guilt. And finally, I became aware of my spiritual commitment to her by recognizing, for the *first* time, the "innocence" (the face of Christ) in her (unfortunately, it was after we were separated). Plus, I never deliberately walked away from her, whether she was in need or not.

⋆   ⋆   ⋆

Suzanne brought me many gifts also. She brought a *gentleness* (the true indication of the Spirit within) I had never known before. She taught me many lessons in giving as she was very generous with material things. An astrologer, when examining our backgrounds together, brought to my attention that our minds were very *joined* (we "thought" a lot alike and had *very* similar life-styles and habits). When it came to being openly, emotionally expressive, no one has ever been able to top her (most people only know how to express *thoughts* and *ideas* not feelings).

Suzanne was also the first one to acknowledge and support my awakening to the presence of God (the Source of Love) in my life. When she was living in San Francisco (our first unprovoked separation) shortly after we had lived together in Salt Lake City for a couple of months, I called her up to let her know about my "first" great revelation. Without even (or ever) mentioning anything about it, Suzanne said, "You just discovered God," to which I said, "Yes!" But, I was mystified by her response because neither of us was religious *at all*, and we never discussed God or anything related to spirituality before. (That summer night in 1979 was the beginning of *my* spiritual turn-around which really took-off when I surrendered my human-ego life in 1982, three months after our annulment, and was my first realization that, in *Love/Truth*, all minds are joined.)

The greatest lesson of our relationship was on a note that I wrote to Suzanne when we *first met* (and she returned to me just before our annulment): "There is *no pride* in love!"

Sauntering...

down the road
with you,
the peacefulness
of our brotherhood
permeates the air,
and the world
joins us in
the contentment
that is it's
very soul.

Roseanne (Cowgirl-Dancer)

At twilight, just before it got dark, I had stopped by my church, which looked like an old fashioned, single room, red brick schoolhouse, in Salt Lake. I had just come from my yoga class at the ashram down the street. Ruth, the minister, asked me to water the front yard; so, I was doing that when the evening class on "Self-esteem" ended and all the students were leaving.

Just before they all left, an attractive young lady with very long, straight, brown hair trailing down her back, large gray-blue eyes and a wonderful child-like smile and sparkle came up to me with my best friend, Mickey, who introduced us.

"Roseanne, this is my good buddy, Jay. How are you doing, brother Jay (a greeting he learned from being raised Mormon, but was indicative of *our* real relationship since he was probably the most 'brotherly' person in my life)?" as this big burly man with sandy-colored hair and full beard gave me a big, loving bear-hug.

I thought she was very attractive, dressed in a short-sleeved polo shirt, tapered-leg faded jeans and white running shoes; but...I did not pursue a relationship with her until almost a year later, because I discovered she was living with another guy for six years.

Later on, Roseanne and I both bought *A Course In Miracles* at the same time from the metaphysical church we regularly attended (separately). I kept hounding her each week during the next year about her progress through it (*it* captured my heart), as it was obvious to me that she *really* loved the *Course* by the way she clutched the three hard-bound books, that made up the set, close to her chest and by the look of *relief* on her face when she first got it.

I didn't realize it then, but this was the beginning of my *first* (of several, I later discovered) "spiritual" relationship where our common bond was our mutual learning of the Truth.

Finally, one Sunday we *both* came to church late and ended up in end-isle seats across from each other, which were rarely available once the service began (we both later acknowledged this as a *sign* that we were *supposed* to get together that day). I was a "leg man" then, and she had *great* legs (she was a perpetual, part-time dance/fine arts student for seven years at the University of Utah in the city), which I couldn't (*chose* not to) keep my eyes off of during the entire service. I asked her to lunch, we *made* love all afternoon and a week later she moved in with me when her male roommate/lover came back from a trip.

For *me*, we had a very different relationship from the *beginning*...beyond the fact that we were "incredible" (her word) lovers together. There was very little, if any, "romance" (drama) in our relationship. We were just *great* friends...my first experience of true *brotherhood* and complete trust with a *woman*. For instance, I came home from work (I was a marketing manager for a telephone company) one evening and shared with her my physical attraction (which always has a "sexual" base to it) I felt for another lady I noticed driving home. I explained that I couldn't understand why I had that urge when I was *completely* satisfied with her (there was none better than her in every respect. I had never been this *open* before...down to the "gut-level.") Roseanne *never* reacted; she was (and still is) *the* most peaceful person I have ever met. There was nothing I could not share with her. Total absence of fear!

We lived together peacefully and contentedly for several months. We exercised, studied spirituality and meditated together early every morning. I came home for lunch (*not* sex) with her every day (she waitressed part-time in the evenings and was a student some afternoons). We traveled, went to plays, concerts and movies and vacationed in the desert together. I won a trip for two to Lake Tahoe, so we even had a honeymoon (although we were never married)...where on my father's birthday, July 14, 1983, we made love non-stop for "9" hours (her orgasms were almost constant)...that was my first *obvious* example of an unexplainable (and, for us, nonrepeatable) event, which to *us* was a "miracle" or a *correction* of our human *perception* because we had never, individually or collectively, experienced anything of that magnitude before.

The sexual act, although it turned out to be *my* "ultimate" fantasy come true on that day, was not what was important. The fact that Roseanne could so "freely" *surrender* herself...because that is what it takes to do what she did...was the miracle, the *gift of Love*. (An orgasm is only a tiny, physical, human expression of "releasing" that precedes our letting go of our male-/femaleness first, our humanness at death secondly and our "individuality"/ego-identity into our formless mind-state ultimately, *if* we are truly going to "surrender" to giving up our *separate* identity, since we don't die, to return to the Christhood of the *one* Son and one Mind of God/Love.)

On the human level, I decided *after* my second wife, Suzanne, that I never wanted to date or get tied-down to a woman who had difficulty having an orgasm (releasing/letting go) again; and, *all* the women I dated regularly up to that point did. Most spiritual partners I've had since Roseanne have been multi-orgasmic and able to expose or look at and share their deep ego fears, guilt and undesirable attributes with me. The two qualities (the ability to release and the ability to be open) *seem* to go together for some reason.

Even though Roseanne and I had the ultimate spiritual and human relationship because we were *great* pals, spiritual partners, playmates, confidants and lovers, I noticed on our last 9-day vacation together in the desert canyons and mountains of southern Utah (my most favorite place on Earth) that she started to "appear" quite sullen at the end. Like a fool, I didn't ask her what the matter was...I just *assumed* that she was unhappy living with me (egos with a "victim" mentality like mine always find fault with our self, first) with no apparent indication until then. I *thought*, "Father, if Roseanne would be happier living with her old boy-friend, let her go back to him. I just want her to be happy." I did not believe that *I* could *help* her solve her unhappiness. I wanted to "run away" rather than help or have to deal with her possible unhappiness with me. I had never learned to understand and face other people's emotional issues and concerns (shades of my parents), and consequently, I had fear in doing so. (It was easier to quit and walk away.)

While we were camping on a mountain at the beginning of the vacation, we awoke one morning, and lying naked on top of our sleeping bag basking in the warmth inside our tent from the morning sun, I began to read a lesson from the *Course* about wanting *only* the "Peace of God"...which we *both* agreed was what we *really* wanted. The next day, as we drove down the mountain, we stopped near the bottom and then two eagles took-off from behind the tall grass *right in front* of our car. We sat there in awe, for what seemed like several minutes, and I felt that God was giving us a sign that we had now become *true* "spiritual" partners to fly together. (Unfortunately, I was too spiritually immature, as mentioned before, to keep my mind focused upon this realization a few days later when she seemed unhappy!)

Well, a couple weeks later she met her old boy-friend one evening and came home *very* late to our place, and I knew, immediately, when she climbed into bed that they had made love (because I knew her so well). I felt angry for what was the *ultimate* deceit; and then, in almost the same instant, I sensed fear from knowing what it was like to lose her forever. In the morning, I told her about my feelings (the most "open" I had ever been) and asked when she was moving back with him. As I told her in that moment, "I am very surprised that I don't *want* to say or do something to you in retaliation for last night. I guess I must *really* love you." (I learned that just being "open" about our feelings, at least to ourselves, and *acknowledging* them *completely* is *all* that is necessary to relieve *any* hurts or fears even though you may *choose* not to "forget" them immediately.)

She moved back with him, but he would not let her talk with me, so she called me from a telephone booth and "cried" (the *only* time she had ever been emotional) because she missed talking (sharing) with me. I was very touched and offered to put her up at my place...I told her that she could sleep on the couch until she could get a place of her own. A few days later, she moved back, and we just fell into our old routine of being spiritual partners and lovers. It was a very open and "easy," peaceful relationship.

Some time (a month or so) later, we went out on a

Saturday night, and feeling so comfortable with each other, we went to separate functions. I wanted to go to some old movie "classics" at the Performing Arts Center, and she wanted to go to the dance recital at the theater. So, *she* dropped me off (since her function ended first) and picked me up...no sense in taking two cars since both events were in the same general area in downtown Salt Lake City. We went for a bite to eat afterwards, and there she was happy to share, what we *both* decided was, a "divine occurrence" (later I learned that all such events are part of our *ego*-script). She met surprisingly, her old boy-friend (yep, the same one!) in the ticket line for the recital...right next to her. They sat together during the concert. *We* took that as a sign that she was to move back with him (see how "egos" can misconstrue *psychic* information and intuition, not realizing that the ego/ human mind sets up these occurrences to distract us from pursuing our "loving" course of living), particularly since I had stopped by my ex-wife's (Suzanne) apartment that afternoon (after not seeing her for two years) to *heal* all unforgiveness from my relationship...*not* get back...with her, which *I* did happily and shared it with Roseanne.

Roseanne left two days later and moved back with him...only she seemed more like his sister who grew up with him for seven years than his lover. We continued to get together a couple afternoons a week as lovers and confidants and spent Sunday mornings in church together for a couple of months. We almost spent Christmas together, but I urged her to take her roommate to her hometown in South Dakota (since they were considering it, and I figured the trip would either make or break their physical relationship, once and for all). I spoke with her and her mother, with whom I had a good telephone rapport, over the holidays and had the impression from what *they* said that Roseanne's relationship with her old boy-friend wasn't very stable...to say the least; but then, neither was *mine* with her (looking back in hindsight).

I invited her to my new townhouse condo, which she picked out with me four months prior, for a New Years Day evening party in 1984; where at the end of the evening, I asked her to marry me and offered to give my home and everything I owned to her. Roseanne literally sank into my arms and told me that she "would live with me in a tent," which I took as a "yes" and was *the* nicest, most unconditionally loving statement anyone had ever made to me (*to this day!*). As she went to her car to return to her boy-friend's place (we agreed that she would tell him the next day of our intentions), Roseanne looked deep into my eyes and said, "Thank you, Father." (We both had a *personal* relationship with God.) I felt like the most blessed person on Earth...I had the *ideal* spiritual partner (I always wanted a classy cowgirl...she was the daughter of a cattleman), a beautiful new home that had *all* the features and characteristics that I ever wanted, a great job working for two loving, caring bosses that I personally liked as friends, the opportunity to live in the most beautiful city surrounded by mountains with the nicest people *in the world* and *several* wonderful and loving friends. On January 1, 1984, I had it ALL, in spades (I thought)!!!

I can't tell you what happened after that except that Roseanne told her roommate two weeks later that she *really* loved me (*we* knew that she loved him, too) and that we decided to be together, again. But...somehow, she decided to move to Seattle, Washington two weeks later to live with an old childhood girl-friend of hers. The morning she left Salt Lake, she called first to say that she wanted to *stop by*, but I told her that I supported *her* decision and wanted her to be happy doing what *she* wanted to do and that she should just go on. (I wonder if I had not been so noble whether we would still be together today?)

As the months rolled on, I missed her terribly. (She kept in frequent contact with her old boy-friend though, who had a toll-free telephone number at work, I found out much later...something about family-type familiarity and security, or our *insecurity*, that must keep drawing us back to the past to finish our learning lessons.) I quit my job to go to a similar job with another company that I got fired from for poor sales performance six months later (I was *tops* in my field the year before). Roseanne suffered from terrible depression (which is nothing more than "self-hatred" from our *ego* when it doesn't get its way) for a long time; was told psychically a number of times about a "man who really loved her," whom she knew was me; and told me that she loved me, but was *unwilling* to have her mind "joined" with mine (which it already was) and felt that I was too needy of her (which was true, but her *absolute* refusal to have anything to do with me spiritually, on this earthly level, shocked me).

I decided to "retire" from the world of *doing* and *having*; and one year later, I gave up my beautiful home and *all* my earthly possessions (except my car and clothes, which weren't much) after a six month semi-recluse period of *only* reading and meditating. I left my nirvana and moved to the central, east coast of Florida.

On two different occasions I was *sent* by two different organizations over the last five years to Seattle for a week or more each time. I believe it was to be available to Roseanne to walk back to our "holy relationship," which she did acknowledge a few years ago, but she never took the opportunity even though I wished she had. So, seven years later, I guess it's over...physically and psychically! (She recently married, finally, at age 31.)

          *   *   *

Looking back, the only fears I could isolate in Roseanne was the time four years ago that she mentioned to me on the phone (we kept occasional contact telephonically over the years) that "love" was a pretty awesome thing and that it could be pretty overwhelming if *accepted* (meaning that one seems to *lose control* of their ego-life). So, I interpreted that as her fear to make a real commitment to a relationship. (I learned much later that when someone who completely understands absolute Truth is around others who don't accept it they have a tendency to "open up" with us; and *our* quiet, unspoken *acknowledgment* of their reality is *our* gift...*not* the "ego" rewards of companionship, etc., that we are used to getting on Earth.) A psychic friend of mine once said of Roseanne, "She needs to be taken care of." Because she was so much like a free spirit in that she had *no* real skills or desire to pursue a career where she could comfortably provide for herself, I could see the truth of my friend's comment. But, Roseanne never seemed to be visibly concerned about being provided for and was one of the most calm people, no matter what, I've ever known. She sauntered, never walked, all the time.

★   ★   ★

Because of Roseanne's (or life's) unpredictable comings and goings, I finally became very uncertain of our relationship and clung to her (rather than letting go) *in my mind* and to the *fantasy* that we would be reunited since I kept being *sent* to Seattle (be careful what you *wish* for...you might get it *without* the "results" *you* expect). I think my realization of her desire/need to be taken care of prompted me to be aware of my own need for the same thing when I moved to Florida. (I see that realization on the human level as a *personification* of the ultimate awareness of my dependence upon God for *everything*.) She held up the mirror of me! I also learned that when Roseanne seemed to need help I was *afraid* to do so because I feared the personal guilt of maybe not being good enough to please her forever. I was also afraid that she would not be my *true* friend, *but* she always called me back whenever I called and left a message. She never avoided me over the years.

★   ★   ★

Roseanne was probably one of the *most gentle* people I've ever known. Whenever she touched me, she felt like a feather, yet she was not particularly delicate being a dancer. She was *very* mellow and peaceful. And, thinking back to our miracle (the ultimate sexual encounter, which *we knew* could have lasted *forever* if someone didn't decide she was hungry), she definitely demonstrated the ability to totally release/surrender. Although our love-*making* (great choice of words since God did not and does not "make" anything or anyone in the world) was *not* "aggressive" or ever done in anger in any way (like after an argument, which we never had), I remember sharing with her during one session when we *first* lived together the feeling that I had that "sex is a form of attack." (Today, I realize that the more my relationship "heals"...becomes like a spiritual brotherhood...with my lover the less desire I have for sex because I feel the need to be very *gentle* with her rather than satisfying my *own* needs and pleasures.)

*   *   *

My *dream* of our reunification over a seven year period told me that *I* could make a lasting commitment and that I took our spiritual brotherhood very seriously. In Roseanne's words, I was her "quintessential cowboy." I also was an example for her of the discipline that it takes to learn and follow the spiritual path, and I know that through the power of love in our "joined" minds (once *one* person realizes their brotherhood with another the relationship becomes "holy") that I helped her telepathically finish a spiritual program that took one year to complete. (Discipline was not her strong point; neither was completion since she went to college part-time for seven years and never completed her degree...but then, neither did my parents, who came *close* but never finished. Do you think there is any truth to the idea that you are *always* finishing or finalizing your relationship with your *parents* in *every* extended boy-girl encounter?? I do...unfortunately, according to my ego!)

       *   *   *

The one human attribute about Roseanne that I did not notice until after we were physically separated for awhile was that she was an "adaptive," meaning that she took on the personality traits of the one most influential friend (hero/idol) in her life at the time. (I realized this in my last spiritual partner, also, three months after we were separated physically.) It's scary when the person you *knew* becomes like the *new* hero/friend in their life. All the *love* you had between you before vanishes in front of your eyes...like it never existed...and you are brought once again to the realization that "this is but a dream." Afterall, *desire* (need) is the "trap" that binds us to Earth. Let go of it, and you will mentally (spiritually) ascend to the awareness (knowledge) of Spirit as *our* essence.

       *   *   *

I guess the *first* real spiritual relationship is like your first kiss...you never forget it!

Constancy

No matter how
I led my life
or what
I didn't do
for him,
my trusty, loving
dog companion
was always there
for me.
His constancy
reminded me
of God,
and hopefully...
me!

Sandy
(Constant
Companion)

One Monday morning in October 1984, I walked out the back door of my townhouse condo in Salt Lake to get into my car in the garage and drive to work. This morning there stood a cute, small, tan colored (with a white underside), terrier-mix, one year old dog with one front paw raised, on my fenced-in back patio, as if to say, "Hi, can I come in?" I patted him on the head and told him what a cute dog he was and clicked the garage door opener. I hopped into my car and drove off.

I came home for lunch at noon-time. After lunch, I walked out the back door to go back to work, and this same dog was standing there again on three legs with front paw raised up and his head bowed. He was really cute, so I went over, shook his paw, patted him on his head, complemented him on having such a cute *act* and told him, "If you are here this evening when I get home, you can come inside." Off to work I went.

When I came home at 5 P.M. guess who was waiting for me? So, I opened the back door into the kitchen and told him to go inside. (I called him Sandy after Little Orphan Annie's dog in the old-time comic strips because he was a dark and light sand-color and he looked like a street orphan. A friend of mine later looked at his paws and said, "This dog has been on the road a long time because the pads on his feet are very calloused.") He sauntered (like Roseanne) through my galley-kitchen and dining room into the living room and hopped up on the couch and layed down, head and all, on his side. I went over to him and told him, without anger, that the furniture was "off limits." I pointed to the landing at the foot of the stairs leading up to the open-loft bedroom on the second floor and said, "Go sleep over there," which he immediately did. Amazing! We had such a *terrific* understanding from the beginning, and he was a very mellow dog. Several of my friends said that Sandy and I were a lot alike (afterall, "like always attracts like"). I recognized our "joining" on the mind level from the very beginning. This was a *very* spiritual relationship.

My next-door neighbor told me later that week that Sandy slept on my back doorstep the prior weekend I was away. Since I was *into* understanding the wonderful way we draw things and people into our life through our consciousness (like minds...expressions of love and "calls for love"...are always drawn together when they are willing to learn the next lessons in their unfoldment), I knew that unconsciously, to my human ego, I called this dog into my life.

I lost my job one week later, so he was great company. I spent the next six months doing absolutely nothing but reading spiritual development books, meditating without music, taking Sandy for a long walk every afternoon along the canal that ran behind my complex, playing solitaire every evening and hosted a "Trivial Pursuit" party once a month at my place. (Sandy loved *adult*-kids as he would *slink* around the floor and go up to *each* person to love them and be patted and stroked while about 12 of us were playing on the carpet. Then, he would come up to me and sit beside me and while facing me he'd put one paw on my shoulder, which meant, "Rub my stomach," and all the women would go, "Ah, isn't he adorable!" I always rubbed his stomach until my hand got tired.)

It wasn't until the *second* week we lived together that I began to see how much alike we were...meaning Sandy "became" more like me (my mirror) from that point on, and I knew that we *always* come together to learn about *ourselves* through others. For instance, whenever I left the house for an hour or more, Sandy removed the seat cushions from my love-seat in the living room where *I* sat all the time and chewed *a* hole in one of them. (This happened three times, and he always chewed the *same* hole larger, which amazed me, until I learned to put him in the back room where there was no furniture. If I put him in the basement, he always shit on the concrete floor, as if to say, "I don't like it down here, so please don't put me here again," so I didn't do that after two times.)

The last time Sandy did this he also knocked over a plant and chewed the cover of a book that I was reading. When I came home, I knelt down on the floor near the debris that he "piled up" as he slinked over to me with his head bowed (he was just like a small child who knew he had done something wrong). I put my hand gently on his head, looked into his tender, dark brown eyes and asked him, "What are you trying to tell me?" Then I "knew" *intuitively*, as I learn most things, that he was holding up the *mirror* of my biggest fear of *being abandoned!* I thanked him, and we never had a problem again. (*Acknowledgment* of what's on the outside is *our* insides, particularly if it causes *any* discomfort, is all that it takes to heal *anything*...provided you look at it *completely*. All relationships require this kind of *work*.)

Our afternoon walks were real special, too. We always went no matter what the weather. Sandy would always stand up on his hind legs whenever I picked up his royal-blue, webbed-nylon leash off of the front door knob. He was like a "camel" because he only *needed* to go out *once* a day and never messed on the carpet the whole time we lived together. (Pretty amazing for a dog that had been on the road for a long time.) He would scamper and remain about 50 feet ahead of me when I undid his leash, but he would glance back to see where I was, constantly. (We were always together, but we gave each other breathing room to be ourselves...whenever I went to someone's office with Sandy to visit or someone came over to my house, he would go off, within eye-sight of me, and lie down...he was a little gentleman!)

One time while we were out on our afternoon sojourn, a *big* black dog, walking with his master, grabbed (bit) Sandy across his *whole* back. When he yelped in pain, I ran and grabbed the other dog by his tail to pull him away, and then his master came and got him off Sandy. (This was my first and *only* experience of ever going to someone's aid in a violent situation, which I abhor. I was glad I did, but I still felt helpless and so sorry for Sandy because he was such a mellow dog, who hardly ever barked and never would provoke another dog or person.) He reminded me in this situation that even though I led a quiet life for the last two years I still felt like a *victim of the world*...and a fear is a "wish" because what we believe or focus on is the way we create how we see and experience our world.

There were three separate nights that Sandy did not come home. The *second* time, I went away the next day before he got home to Phoenix, Arizona for four nights, and he slept on my front doorstep while I was gone. The *third* time was the night before I left Utah for Florida (my two kids called and pleaded with me to come and rescue them from their mother), which was wonderful because I would have been torn apart if I had to look into his "soul-ful" eyes that would have plucked at my heart when I drove off early the next morning. (It came to me that that is why my soul-mates *left me*, because *I didn't* want to leave them; and yet, I needed to move on to share my life with others and complete my own learning. As much as I would like to find a "home" on Earth, I seem to be a "world traveler," as one friend put it...just like Sandy, who left the home we were staying in three days after I did.)

Sandy *never* liked to ride in the car, no matter what...he always threw-up (a friend said it was because he was probably dropped-off somewhere away from his home when he became a street orphan). I left him with my best friend's oldest son, who I was training to take Sandy for walks and having him feed him the last week I was there. But, Sandy *always* slept at my feet.

Sandy was the *most* unconditionally loving essence (maybe that's why a dog is G-o-d spelled backwards) in my life. (If I dwell on him, I miss him terribly.) But...I would not submit him to the fleas down here (he never had even *one*), which are rampant in the Florida grass (everything is prolific here). So, I left him where I thought he would be cared for and the most comfortable. I *hated* leaving my spiritual partner behind, but I had to move on. Human life *always* involves pain when we have to leave the ones we love (maybe...it's need). God would never have done this to us!

"Goodnight, Sandy, wherever you are! I secretly (?) hoped that you would have walked 2700 miles and *found me* like you did in the beginning. *Then* I would never leave you, which I never have in my heart...the only place it really matters! Such innocence I see in your eyes, even now (loved ones *never* die as long as we remember them)."

The Unknown Mystic

Without ever
realizing it
yourself,
you are
a "mystic"
hiding behind
the facade
of your
addictions
to your
human ego
until...
I came along
and looked
into the
mirror
of you
and saw
my own
reflection.

Connie
(Caribbean Queen)

When I moved to Palm Bay, Florida (half way down the east coast), my insurance company assigned me to a local agent. When I walked in to change my policy, there was this service representative there (one of two) that my new agent assigned me to. Her name was Connie, and she was "naturally" beautiful as she wore no makeup and looked like a young Elizabeth Taylor with very gentle and peaceful eyes. I was dumb-founded. All I could do was stare at her, and she stared at me, too.

Later, we *both* recognized that it was part of *the* universal plan that we meet (I now know that "we," not God as so many believe, create our world ourselves by drawing to us "like minds"/people with similar needs and learning lessons) because there was another insurance agent from the same company much closer to my townhouse condo...and, my new agent gave me to *her* rather than the service representative who ordinarily would have handled me (I was in her part of the alphabet). I didn't understand it then, but I had fallen across one of the most mystical people in my life.

I didn't ask her out, but later that week I ran into her one evening with her five year old daughter in a drug store near my *new* home, which didn't have a refrigerator yet. I asked her if I might store some perishable food at her place for a short while. She said, "Sure," and so, later that week I went over to her home in a trailer park with some items to put in her refrigerator, which I offered to share with her.

When I went to her home the first time, I was mesmerized by the quiet, sultry, innocent look in her light blue eyes and the peacefulness of her demeanor...and the look of her cotton dress and barefeet, with her legs draped across the arm of the deep cushioned chair she was sitting in, like a caribbean queen. She was real *layback*, as I was.

We talked right away about spirituality (my favorite topic), so I knew that this woman was *special*. As a matter of fact, *she* carried most of the conversation, which was a first for me. When I started to share some of my philosophical insight with her, she silenced me and said, "I need you to just listen, because I need you to be a sounding board while *I* teach *myself* about these spiritual things." I knew then I was in the company of a real *mystic* (and yes, it takes one to know one) and one who I looked forward to having as a long-term friend...not a lover.

I found the "innocence" in her *so powerful* that the

thought of having a boy-girl, romantic relationship with her didn't occur to me (regardless of how attractive she was) until one afternoon. I took her with me and my 17 year old daughter, Lisa, to a friend's house built out over a pond. Connie and I talked for a long time about her 13 year alcohol and drug addiction (she was 26 then). She talked and I listened, as usual. (Having just given up my eight year periodic-addiction to marijuana, I could see "in" her *my* innocence as I forgave *my self* by this recognition. You always forgive yourself by recognizing *your* ego-self in someonelse!) Just before we finished, she leaned over and kissed me on the lips. I was touched, and she was very beautiful and comfortable to be with...but, I couldn't (for some unknown reason) look at her *as just a woman*, so I didn't follow-through on the *physical* aspect of our relationship until six weeks later.

I don't remember what happened exactly, but we were *both* on our knees on her kitchen floor one evening, and she planted *the* most passionate kiss on my lips in my entire life. ("Passion" means *to suffer*, so...passionate people are *desperate* people who are "suffering" from a lack of love. But, I didn't realize that back then.) One kiss led to another, and quickly we became gentle, but passionate lovers. (Looking back on *all* of my spiritual, special-love relationships, I was *never* the one to *initiate* it! This is the part that has always baffled me; every one of them decided, before me, that *they* wanted to have a relationship with me because of my "spirituality"...yet, as you will see, *every* one of them left me. Mind transfer happens all the time, and people are not aware of the power of their "feelings" and "attitudes," not necessarily their thoughts, that draw them together and affect each other, and the universe.)

I once thought about my relationship with Connie while I was with her, "Why are you (Jay), a spiritual seeker, in a relationship with this addict?" The answer came to me that whether she was sober or not, listening to her was like listening to God, *Himself*. The most incredible understanding of *absolute* Truth came out of her mouth. She "knew" (without *ever* reading or studying) *everything* that I had read and studied about the Truth for the previous two years. What happened, I found out almost immediately after asking Spirit (my, and our, higher Self) how this could be, was (I was intuitively *told*) that Connie's and my mind had "joined" so that everything that I had learned intellectually had *transferred* to her mind (meaning that she could then tap into the *same* universal mind that I was part of). I had learned it *for* her. (This is how the world is "getting it" now and will *totally* understand the Truth and be a place of peace and brotherly love in the *near* future!) Truth/ Love transfers between all minds that are open or "willing" to receive it. *Feeling* does everything, and intellectual thinking and understanding does nothing, "in reality."

I remember sitting with Connie in her living room one night after she had gotten drunk and stoned (I never once in the time we were together asked her to stop) and asking God, silently, to give *me* the strength to get through this and to help her. **He** did, and miraculously, three months after our relationship began, she stopped drinking and smoking dope for the *first time* in 13 years. After Connie stopped, we went to her family reunion that summer in North Carolina and even though her brother, sister, brother-in-law and cousins were all smoking dope and drinking beer out on the pontoon boat in the lake (I cringed at the thought), *she* did *not*! Miracle of miracles!

Connie played out for me *my* most romantic-side. One evening, on July 22, 1985, after she had been sober for awhile, Connie took me to the most adorable, romantic, very small, white chapel with stained-glass windows and shaped like a cross (from above), surrounded by a beautiful lawn and palm trees and situated between, and close to, a river *and* the ocean. Well, we sat and talked on the chapel steps for quite awhile. As we stood up, late in the evening, to go home, Connie put my hands inside of hers in an upward, prayer position and, with those quiet, dream-like eyes of hers, looked silently, longingly and deeply into my heart. (I gulped...because I was scared by what I heard *her* heart asking me to do...to commit to her, forever.) So, with my voice breaking (for the *first* time in a romantic setting), I said looking deep into her eyes, "I would be very pleased if you would marry me." She then said without blinking, "And I, would be very pleased if you would marry me." We walked happily and with quiet reverence back to the car. (I don't ever remember being *nervous* before...I had been married twice previously... when I asked someone to marry me. Could it be that I picked up her and my fear of *total* surrender, which I knew I would do for Connie, and perhaps had never loved another this deeply before!)

The next day *I* went and picked out, without her, the most precious diamond-encircled wedding band and put it on my American Express card. I wasn't working at the time and had very little money. (Connie brought out every last drop of generosity I had inside. There was nothing I wouldn't have given her.) That evening when she got through work, I slipped it on her finger, and it fit perfectly. She loved it and was touched deeply because no one had ever given her a diamond ring (and *I* had never done so before). It made me very happy to do for her. *She* picked a date for us to marry that was about three or four weeks from then.

We never got married as she left *her* house where we were both living on *the day* she picked for us to do so and disappeared for three days. I didn't know where she had gone. It was one of the most bizarre experiences of my life. (Alcoholics and drug addicts are *very* spiritual people, usually unbeknownst to themselves, which causes them to feel disoriented in this physical world, and that is why they turn to an outside substance to ease their pain from feeling out-of-place. Because of that crazy disorientation, they frequently do unpredictable, involuntary or bizarre things until they learn to honor, surrender to and obey their true spiritual nature. Marry or live with one, and you'll learn to let go of *your* "controlling" nature, which everyone's ego is, because they are uncontrollable. Forgive/overlook their condition, and they are healed...if you can love the Spirit of them.)

On the positive side, Connie didn't become an

addict again, and I was glad to be a (maybe large) part of her releasing her outward dependency. I was dependent upon my desire ("need") to continue our relationship (as I was with all of them) because I couldn't believe that people with holy relationships (where they recognize their *wholeness* rather than ego-dependencies) should separate unless it was the final transition. I have since learned otherwise. Any investment in "things," to include *spiritual* relationships, keeps me, and us, trapped in the *dream* called the "illusion of life" on Earth.

Since she had begun to get out from underneath the control of her *ego*-dependency (the *belief* that we are only a human being is the addiction of all addictions) when we separated, it wasn't clear why we were parting, particularly since we *both* acknowledged that we felt like we were losing our *best friend*. But, I did have this sense, which is what "vision" is, that I had completed *my* function in her life.

It seems that I came to Earth to help people cleanup their *personal* "projects" (I even started in the business world in *project* management)...their *stuff* that they need to "forgive" themselves and others for, that they *thought* they had or had not done to and for each other. (I guess that's a pretty nice thing to be able to do for people, but tell my ego that as *it* jumps and screams, "That's not enough...what about what *I* want!?" Too bad...time to grow up!)

*   *   *

The only fear I can isolate in Connie as being the *symptom* (*not* cause, since *we* are the "cause" of *everything* that happens in our life) of why our relationship did not continue was that Connie was not ready to *totally* surrender her ego to making a 100% commitment (a mirror-image of my past, again). Nor was she willing to surrender losing *ego*-control of her life. My mere *presence* in her life would remind her, "What are you doing playing in the sandbox (being an earthling)?" Even though she told me in the beginning that she called me into her life because she was ready for a relationship with a *spiritual* man (and ended up with a "holy" man dedicated to walking the path to *wholeness* of Self realization), she listened to her *ego* and walked back into world (mentally). Connie confided five years later that she thought my diet (primarily bread and water) was "too kooky" for her and that she liked "fitting in" rather than being different than everyonelse, which she thought I did. (We are so afraid of taking that last step in our "total" commitment to *living* the Truth, *believing* in our higher Self as our true reality, for fear that "we" won't exist anymore. The funny thing about all this is that the "human-ego" that *fears* isn't even us! We are the formless Spirit that exists *behind* our physical facades.)

*   *   *

My fear was that I could not depend on Connie because of her unpredictable (although infrequent) behavior, which left me with great feelings of uncertainty about the viability of a *forever* relationship with her in *any* form on the earthly level. My feeling was that *both* parties had to be committed to forgiving themselves and everyonelse in order for the union to survive.

*   *   *

I did learn to be *totally* giving and willing to make a spiritual commitment to Connie, who brought me the ultimate *romantic* encounter and great peacefulness (she could do absolutely "nothing" for the longest time...just sit and listen to the universe...very mellow!). She also had great patience with everyone. Our relationship was the most mystical, up to that point, in my life.

*   *   *

There was a remake of the movie, The Razor's Edge, which seemed like a replay of our relationship (since I saw it after Connie and I separated). I watched it on TV with my daughter, Lisa, who agreed. It was the story of a young man who went to Europe to be a Red Cross ambulance driver during World War I. He becomes disenchanted with life on Earth because of the horror of war and goes off to the Far East, to what seems like Tibet, to learn the truths of spiritual life. After he goes to the mountain top there to learn the Truth (like I did when I went to Salt Lake City, which is surrounded by mountains), he burns his books when he finally *realizes* "It." He comes back to *normal* life and becomes a street vendor in Paris, where he meets an old girl-friend from school in America, who has become a prostitute to support her alcohol and heroin habit. He takes her home with him; and in three months (the same time it took

-53-

Connie), he helps her get "straight" (off the booze and drugs). The movie ends shortly after the girl gets killed (she walked back into her *old* ego-world) and he says, "I thought she was my *reward*" (as I thought Connie was) for attaining spiritual enlightenment. He goes back to America to just "be."

I realized at the end of the movie that is *all* I and any of us are here to do...just *be*, which doesn't mean we have to die or fade from Earth. Having a special, *spiritual*, boy-girl relationship is *not* the "epitome" of achieving spiritual realization in the world, but *any* two people, or more, *sharing* the mutual realization of their "Spirit" (Christhood) is!

★   ★   ★

Connie once signed a birthday card to her daughter, "Connie, alias Mom." She *knew* inside her heart that she was *more than* just a mother to her daughter...she understood the brotherhood of Spirit. Without ever acknowledging it her self, she was a mystic (hiding amongst the *normal* people).

Cool As Ice, Warm As Toast, Never Missed A Trick

It never ceases
to amaze me
how you can be
cool as ice
when you're involved
in business or projects;
and then, switch again,
and become
warm as toast...
all-*thoughtful*
and giving,
beyond *anyone I've known;*
you never missed
a trick...
you saw every
"slightest" thing
I did for you.
(Thank you...
it's nice
to be appreciated!)

Robilee
(Business Woman)

After my relationship ended with Connie, a male friend of mine from church called me up on the telephone and told me that his son in California had become a cocaine addict and that he didn't know what to do about it...but, someone had suggested that he go to a "support group" meeting tonight, and he asked me if I'd like to go. I said, "Sure...why not!"...I was always up for experiencing any wholesome activity.

The meeting turned out to be an "Al-Anon" meeting (for families and partners of alcoholics/drug addicts following the tradition of the 12-step Alcoholics Anonymous program), which was more loving and spiritual because of the large number of people who had come together to *openly* share with, help and support one another than any church I had ever been to (and, I had been to quite a few at that point). I kept going back for the love (*acceptance*) and the hugs (they were very unafraid to reach out and touch each other).

I met this tall, attractive brunette named Robilee there. Her two ex-husbands had been alcoholics, the ones who play *victim* to the *controller*-role of their partners. (A year later, I told this group that I spent the first 21 years of my life playing victim and the next 21 years *playing* controller, and of the two, I preferred to be a victim. So, I began attending and *enjoying* the camaraderie of the addicts *more* in Alcoholics Anonymous, AA, meetings, and I no longer drank or took drugs then. They were much more open than the "controllers" in Al-Anon.)

Robilee was a reserved, professional business woman, which coincided nicely with my past, business executive/professional *role* and my current position in administration at the local community college. We went out together for three months before I ever kissed her or even held her hand (not exactly your typical romantic relationship, but we did share the recognition of *exposing* one's ego-self to *release guilt* as *we* did together at the Al-Anon meetings). We went for long walks on the beach together one night a week (she lived far north of me), and she would always hold onto me very closely. Sometimes we would stand hugging each other for fairly long periods of time (10 - 30 minutes).

The first time we went out she sat on the stairway leading down to the beach in Melbourne (Florida) near where I lived, and I stood in the sand facing her, with a full moon rising over my shoulders, talking. She confessed (while I was hugging her in a standing position for 30 minutes) that she had had an orgasm just "thinking" about me driving her car home one evening. (I guess I should have realized right then, and *remembered* later, that this person was *deep* into visual images and body/idol worship rather than spiritual realization, much like *I was* prior to learning the Truth...another big opportunity to forgive *myself*.) We did not become lovers that night even though we talked until dawn. It felt like a great friendship though, as she was so *open* about her opinions and thoughts. I enjoyed just *being* with her.

Finally, one evening, three months later, at a Christmas party at her boss' house I happened to kiss her on the lips, and Robilee stood there transfixed with her eyes closed. I wondered why *I* kissed her because I felt more like her *brother* than anything. When I took her home, she had me wait in the living room (without any lights on) while she went and took a shower. When Robilee came out with just a towel wrapped around her into the darkened room, I gulped and thought, "Please, let me be able to *please* this lovely woman." (I was so locked into a holy consciousness after my experience with Connie that it was difficult for me to respond in a normal, *human* way.)

When she took off her towel moments later in the bedroom, there seemed like a golden mist or *veil* covered her entire body in my *vision*. It was a very mystical experience for *me* (she did not have any similar awareness herself), and I *felt* a great reverence for this person as my holy brother. (Yes, we did *make* love, but we can't "create" love *physically*.) We became great lovers (she was multi-orgasmic because of her incredible, visual imagination) until our peaceful relationship ended *abruptly* three months later on *my* birthday without *any* warning (which was the last time I saw her since she cut-off all personal, written and telephonic communication with me shortly afterwards). I did have a "feeling" that day that I'd never see her again.

While we were together for those six months, I had an interesting realizaton. One of my associates at the college where I was working was a female professor who reminded my very much of my first wife in *attitude* and *demeanor*, which years ago I promised to never be "around" again. We had a very short, very torrid affair in her office one week after I made love to Robilee (seems that experience opened up Pandora's box for me). Robilee, on the other hand, reminded me of my mother's ego by her detached, professional behavior, which I hated. I had introduced Robilee to my cohort, and they seemed to get along well (they each were raising a very loving son of the same age) and had swapped phone numbers.

The interesting aspect of this was that I felt sand-wiched sexually (and sex is usually the *draw* that brings men and women together to work out their past with the other person that they *represent*...like family members and former partners) between my ex-wife and mother. I was hearing this voice saying, "See...all we do is keep *replaying the past* until we learn to forgive/overlook it without any emotional reaction. Robilee and your co-worker are your mother and ex-wife, respectively, and it's like watching children in the sandbox reenacting your past isn't it?!" It sure was!

Well, Robilee ended our relationship in a mystical way, as I heard her on the telephone that evening say, "Jay, don't take this *personal*. You are very loving and giving (my second wife said the same thing to me on the telephone on her wedding day to her third husband), but I choose to be apart from you now for awhile." My ego *did* take it personal, of course, but my higher (real) Self, inside my mind, told me that she was just coming from Spirit and was telling me that my job was finished with *her*...and, it was time to move on and let go of our relationship in the physical realm. My ego, as usual, was *addicted* to her physical and sexual presence, so it was a good thing I had my "AA" meetings to go to where we learned that a problem in dealing with life had *nothing* to do with alcohol or drugs but "self" (meaning our ego). The earthling part of us wants to love and feel loved (BUT, it's really *need*), and there is nothing like the support and acceptance (i.e. "real" love) of others *until* you can rely totally on your *own* higher Self!

*   *   *

The only thing that Robilee seemed to fear was "being controlled" by *any* authority figure, like her father, and making a 100% commitment in a relationship. Nor, did she like *seeing herself* in my mother as she recognized some of their not so pleasant similarities. (I guess our minds were more joined than I realized as she learned this insight with me, I was told intuitively. Actually, she *once* acknowledged that there were several instances that she was aware that our minds were *one*, which seemed to frighten her and her ability to be *singularly* "in control" of her life. Of course, my *ego*, as well as everyone's, wants that. But then, "it" is *not* us, and we are all in this together since *all* minds are joined!)

*   *   *

Robilee always moved fast physically and was so *determined* in what she wanted to do that I oftentimes felt over-powered (controlled) by her. (A mirror image of *my* past businessman role!) She seemed preoccupied with *her* control over life, to the point that I and her 10 year old son didn't matter *many* times. I thought she treated her son very impersonally, which frightened me, by always calling him "son" rather than by his name, so much so that she *acted* like an authority-figure (probably her dad). She also got *very* angry with her son over small things (and he was a very mild-mannered kid), which reminded me of growing up with my mother, unfortunately.

Because of her intense self-concern, you can imagine how "uncertain" I always felt in our relationship. I remember my mother saying, "You two spent more time avoiding loving each other." (I saw my mother begin to accept the concept of "it takes one to know one" shortly thereafter...and was hoping that she *saw herself* in Robilee, who she once called "Lady Cool.") So, I learned that Robilee held up my mirror image (and my mother's) of just how selfish and ego-centered *my* ego was in the past about having its own way in everything. "Bless you, Robilee!"

Robilee was probably one of the *most* "thoughtful" people I've ever known. For instance, when my mother talked about a Barbra Streisand tape she wanted in her presence, Robilee went out, bought it and mailed it to her (for no reason or personal gain); and she sent me flowers when I was ill in bed at home for only a day. She loved to go for slow walks and to ride with me in the car, because she *loved* our peaceful, quiet-time together. She was not the slightest bit "mouthy" or nervous although she had tremendous high energy, which she burned-off working out at a fitness center several days a week.

I know I was the first (as with *all* my other spiritual partners...and maybe this was my purpose in life) to introduce and demonstrate *the* Truth for her that God did not create the physical universe (*we* did, by "imaging" it in), which is a big hurdle to climb over when you've been told otherwise for so long by your parents, ministers and the world, as a whole. I believe that I was spiritually committed, more than anything, to our relationship. I even saw her hug and kiss her ex-husband one night, after many years of not seeing him and being very bitter towards him, when he came to pick up their son for the evening. (It was great "seeing" that my *consciousness* could reach others and bring peace and forgiveness into their lives!)

A Poet's Lament

How many times
have I been
down this road?
Each time
I thought
I'd die
of a
"broken heart."
Since we
choose the way
we leave the earth,
I guess
this *could*
be mine.

Josephine
(Southern Belle)

Two and a half years had passed since I had a significant woman in my life after Robilee. One night in October 1988, I went to a spiritual study group at a friend's high-rise condo near the beach (an hour or so north of my home in Jupiter, Florida). I noticed a very attractive young lady with short red hair sitting on the couch (I used to hate red-headed women because I thought they always looked so pale and sickly). Since her hair was all teased-out, which dated her, and her clothes made her look sort of "trashy" (my *ego* always found trashy-looking women the most sexy...and she was...yes, you're right... my ego is *very* judgmental about female bodies), I thought that she wasn't my type.

Later after the meeting broke up and everyone was milling around in the kitchen, I walked up to her, found out her name was Josephine ("Jo" for short), looked into her eyes and saw the *most* tender, loving, "innocent" look (the face of Christ) I had ever seen in an *adult* and gave her a big hug, which she returned gracefully and lovingly. (Looking back two years ago to that moment, I can say that I *always* loved her very deeply in a very *spiritual* way that can't be described...but it was like meeting God inside yourself. This person brought that out in *me*, which I never fully realized until now.)

I never thought about asking her out even though I had seen her again at other gatherings. (She later told me that she kept trying to get my attention so that I would.) Then three months later, I saw her again one evening at a friend's Christmas party. Jo was elegantly attired in a beige, crocheted two-piece dress with matching thin-strapped pumps that made her look very sophisticated. I walked over to her, and she just glowed and seemed so happy to see me and greeted me as a southern belle would.

We walked into the family room like two "long lost" lovers arm-in-arm, and when I hugged her (I couldn't resist the way she looked so deep into my heart), we began dancing *without* any music because my "ego" felt embarrassed that our *mutual* love for each other was *so obvious to everyone* that *it* urged me to take her into the living room away from them. *She* kissed me gently on the lips twice and kept looking so longingly and deeply into my eyes (I could see the innocence of the world in them). I became scared because no one had ever been this *open* with me before. It was perfect, innocent love meeting itself. (The power of love...and the *call* for it...still reverberates in my mind from that encounter, after all this time.) My ego was really fearful that we might create a "scene" by our display of love and affection for each other, so I suggested that we leave, which we did.

I do remember hearing *very gently* in my mind, "You can marry her tonight"...but, I ignored the thought (although I *really* believed that we would marry someday, and I can't tell you why). We drove around for awhile (I secretly thought about flying to Nevada to get married that evening.) When I finally parked the car and looked into her eyes again, I saw such a happy innocence twinkling in them (literally) that I *knew* I could *never* take advantage of this person, sexually or otherwise. (I have never felt such *pure* love, to this day!) She was like an angel, and I knew that I would *always* "love" her. Because I was staying with another friend, I couldn't take her home with me; and because she had company at her place, I just brought her home and left.

Since I worked, and later moved quite a ways south from her after the party, I only talked to Jo on her toll-free business number that she *told* me to call. Once, I stopped by for a short while early on a Saturday morning and caught her without her makeup on and in her housecoat, but I didn't care (I really adored her *essence* beyond her physical appearance). I continued to phone her occasionally at work as I was traveling around the country with my job until the following April, when it ended abruptly without any warning.

Not knowing what to do at that point and not having a place to live (my housemate in West Palm Beach decided she wanted her house to herself at the same time

I lost my job), I drove north on a Friday evening and stopped at Jo's. She was meeting with a fellow who was going to lead her band if she went back into professional singing again. She invited me in, told me on the sly that I could go with them (I thought he was her boy-friend) that evening to check out some other band at a local night club, and that I was welcome to spend the night on her couch. I said, "Sure" since I had nothing else to do and no where in particular to go.

At the night club, Jo and I danced for the first time (to music) like we were *glued* to each other and had been dancing together for some time. The other fellow never danced with Jo, and I discovered that he really wasn't her boy-friend. When we came back to her townhouse apartment, I slept alone on the couch .

The next day (Saturday) we puttered around doing her errands, as I had none, and went that evening to see the movie, Field of Dreams, where this man and his red-headed wife (Jo noticed many similarities between us and them) plow under a portion of their cornfield to turn it into a baseball field because he hears a "voice" *internally* that tells him to do so. Jo said, "It's happening!" at that point (meaning that the *world* is catching on to inner spiritual guidance...because movies show us our consciousness as it currently *is*), and tears rolled down my cheeks. I was speechless with *relief* that the *world* was beginning to understand the Truth. We came home, and Jo gave me her bed upstairs while she stayed downstairs on the couch (she didn't want her daughter to wake me up when she came home later).

On Sunday, I met her 19 year old daughter, and we hit it off (I had a 21 and a 18 year old daughter). I had two really nice conversations with her that day about absolute Truth...once with a gay, male friend of hers in the evening. Her daughter and her friend continued to talk on the couch in the living room, so *she* suggested I go up to her mother's room with Jo. Since it was late and we were both tired, we went to bed. It was the first time we made love (courtesy of her daughter). The next morning Jo went to work, and I drove an hour north to my parents' to stay in their townhouse condo.

Since I was told the previous year that I *belonged* in Australia by an older woman from there that I met at a conference on *real* spiritual healing, I felt compelled to go. When I went to my parents' house, I immediately started applying for a visa and inquiring about emigration information from Australia. I thought, as did my dad, that I was going there to live. (My parents told me later that they didn't think I would come home even though I had a return ticket.) It was a very confusing time. I didn't have any idea where I was going and what I was going to do. I was supposed to go to Australia though, according to my intuition. (To this day, I don't know why I went other than to heal their minds, which is what happens *wherever* I go.) Even though I loved Jo, my preoccupation with my quest kept her out of my mind. I left about four weeks later.

I stopped in Los Angeles to go on a week-long cruise of the Mexican Riviera with a female friend who arranged the super-inexpensive trip for $150. I did nothing but find fault with her the whole time (we really were too different personality types), so we took separate tours of the Mexican countryside when the ship docked. It was nice to be able to visit with the Mexicans as that is my favorite thing to do (just *visit* with all the people in the *world*...because wherever I go the Holy Spirit remains to help heal their minds by bringing more Love into their awareness...just like Jesus said).

Then I flew to Australia with a three day stop-over in Auckland, New Zealand, which I loved. (Coming back, I stopped on Kauai, Hawaii, which I later decided was where I wanted to live, because it had everything I had in Florida, plus mountains and a red-dirt canyon that I dearly missed from living out West.) Well, believing that I was going to move to Australia, at first, I combed all over the countryside and all through the major cities and climbed her biggest mountain-like rock. I walked 12 - 14 hours a day, wherever there were people. I looked into starting a business there and for employment in its colleges and universities. In the two months that I was there, I only found a couple of women attractive (and I was surrounded by *lots* of women in their twenties, in particular, in the youth hostels I stayed in all over), but the memory of Josephine just kept haunting me ever so gently all throughout my stay there (like she was *supposed to be* my spiritual partner).

When I came home, I stopped at two old girl-friends' before going to Jo's. I was *scared* to surrender to the thought of having my *ultimate* spiritual partner on the *earth level*. (God/Love is *the* "ultimate" relationship!)

When I arrived at Jo's, she was dressed the *same as I* in khaki shorts (the *first* shorts she ever owned, at 44) and white jersey top. She was all smiles, and immediately proceeded to tell me how *awful* she felt that I might never be coming back and how much she missed me when I went away. (I was very surprised!) Then she showed me her hands. She had *long* fingernails for the *first* time in her life. I told her that was the *only* thing I thought she was lacking physically before I left the country and that the "joining" of our minds *in Spirit (Love)* "allowed" it to happen. She thanked me with a big hug. (I think back now and realize that we never had a romantic relationship as such, because I was *afraid* of really letting go in a child-like way of total abandonment, which Jo could do.)

Well, as time progressed and we went from summer to fall to winter, Jo and I spent almost every weekend together from Friday evening to Monday morning, when she went back to work. There were *three* times (like my other relationships) that *she* wanted to cut-off our relationship for *no reason*, after which she confided to me that she was glad I stayed. (I always felt like I was being tested to see if I could stand up under the pressure of her *ego*, which was clearly trying to destroy our relationship...as *it* is in *all* of us! The ego "wins" when two people are separated.)

I remember Jo saying once, "I'm sorry I'm so boring. All I ever want to do is stay home (in the evenings)." Well, having done everything I ever wanted to do and having been every place in the world that I ever wanted to be (Jo had, too), I told her that I definitely was not bored with her. (I thought *I* was boring for her until she said that...*or* did she just read my mind and play it back for me?) I was always the *happiest* (most peaceful) just "being" with her. We never had to *do* anything.

To just *be* with Jo was heaven on Earth for me until I *felt guided* to leave Florida in February 1990. At that time, even though we had agreed the past summer to marry at some point, my *ego* felt very "needy" of having something (conventionally) constructive and worthwhile to do and a way to "provide" for *us* since I had been unemployed for 10 months. And, I wanted Jo to be more openly committed to our relationship and be *able* to spend more time with me. (She was working 12 - 14 hours a day, 6-7 days a week as the Controller and "number two" person of her company, which was half way through its six month busy season...it was like living with myself when I was a young businessman and had little time for love and my family...not a pleasant image of my past; but then, like in Charles Dicken's A Christmas Carol with Scrooge looking at his horrible personality, our *close* personal relationships are supposed to hold up *our* mirror...and Jo sure did.)

Feeling like I was unwanted and unneeded (see how the ego blows things way out of proportion?!), I packed my few belongings a week after my dad told me that I would have to leave his house within two months and left for Salt Lake City (which was the *only* place that felt like a "spiritual home" for me on Earth). I *needed* desperately to feel loved, but was not aware that that was what I wanted at the time. So, I thought, "I know the city well, loved the scenery and the people...why not live there until something comes along for *worthwhile* employment, and then, I could send for Jo?" (but...I never told her this. I realized much later that *I* needed to be "rescued" as *proof* that she "really" loved me like Jo did when she attempted to walk away from our relationship! We often confuse *need* and *being rescued* with love.)

After two months of daily, hard work there to finish typing and editing four books on my birthday, April 6, I called Jo the day after her birthday (one week later) to wish her well and tell her that I loved her. Since she acted very light-hearted (almost "flaky") and because I wanted to talk with the *real* her, not her ego-act, I ended the conversation early. I called every couple of weeks over the next two months. Each time, she acted like a happy-go-lucky kid (which is very nice when you've looked at *all* your ego-stuff and have no more *hidden* anger...as *most* "effervescent" people do!...otherwise, it's just a cover-up) *not* her *real*, sweet, quiet, *gentle* Self (that I admit could have been an *imitation* of me when I was physically around since I could see while I was gone that she was an "adaptive" personality. Jo had told me previously that by the end of her 10 year second marriage she felt like she had *lost* her own identity, and I didn't want that to happen with us.)

(NOTE: People are not aware that *all* minds are joined and that all *thought* takes form some place in the universe. Therefore, we *all* become "adaptives" of each other on the ego-level. So, when parents caution their children about keeping "good" company with the right friends, they are unknowingly teaching them about mind transfer, which goes on all the time. *We* imitate and absorb unconsciously from the ones we love...or, should I say "idolize.")

During our last pleasant telephone conversation two months later, Jo told me that although she thought she had forgiven a long-term hurt with her father she recently discovered that she hadn't. About a week later, I was lying on the couch one evening by myself at a friend's house, 2700 miles away from Jo in Salt Lake City, when all of a sudden this thought *came into my mind* while I was busy reading that said, "She (meaning Jo) was just like her father, who was very mouthy and bossy (which she could have realized if she acknowledged what *she* sounded like on her choral rehearsal tapes), was a manipulator/controller (which she could have acknowledged by looking at the 'controllable' men she chose to date in her recent past as well as her job title) and was not a 'finisher' (which was evident from the fact that she had almost completed her college degree, but for some reason *would* not)." I had only experienced these *ego* traits "indirectly" from things that she had *told me* about herself.

I lay there on the couch for awhile, stunned, when all of a sudden this *inner-knowingness* said, "Get up and write it down before you forget," which I did as I *scrambled* to find a notepad. I very quickly dashed the information down, but I forgot the last item about "finishing" until much later. I put some additional explanatory information about myself in the letter because I realized that *I also* had hidden guilt for these *same* qualities and stated that I wanted to trust that I could tell her *anything* from that point on as we both had shared our similar, deepest, darkest, most guilt-producing secret together. (We had been verbally, physically and sexually abused while in vulnerable, "child-like" *states of mind*, which can come and go at *any* point in your life.)

As I told Jo in the letter, I could now see these traits in her because *I* had been very talkative (insecure and needy) and bossy (demanding); I used to be a manipulator by pursuing women for my sexual pleasure who were playing *victims* (like me) and were very needy or emotionally weak; and whenever a serious love relationship began to have difficulties, I would avoid dealing with the woman's concerns and *any* "emotional" confrontation out of fear and not "finish" or complete our relationship. (Mirror images of each other!!)

I was working then in a hospital, so I stopped in the gift shop to buy three postage stamps for three letters I had to mail (including what might be considered an unpleasant or *revealing* one for Jo). The older woman volunteer who was running the place that day had only "two." So, I took that as a "sign" (a psychic message...which I don't usually pay attention to) that I was *not* supposed to send Jo the letter with the exposure of her worst *ego* traits (which we *all* have to look at in order to go BEYOND ALL FEAR). I left it in my pocket and mailed the other two.

Later on that morning, the lady from the gift shop saw me in the hall and tracked me down and said, "Here's the other stamp you wanted, sir." I gulped because I felt like I was supposed to mail the now *infamous* letter (do you see how "fear" acts like a *wish*, a desire, in bringing into our life what we think about?!). I thanked her, put the stamp on the letter and inserted it in the mailbox. I wished Jo well, in thought, because I knew it is tough to really acknowledge the "seeming" horribleness (but un-reality) of our ego-*act*. To have someone there (if you can't turn to Spirit) to share with who will *always* love you (as I had demonstrated to Jo) can help ease the burden.

Guess what happened when Jo got the letter? Guess what consciousness (Spirit or ego) she was in when she did? You guessed it! I forgot her ego was part "Irish." She must have *exploded*, because three days later I received the *briefest* phone call of my life one evening, spoken so fast and angrily that I almost couldn't hear the words. ("Rage" was also a major characteristic of her father that she was trying to learn to forgive...anger is nothing more than a *mask* to cover-up the guilt we *accept* inside our mind and an attempt to project or blame the person that exposes it as being a *fault finder*...and we always *do* what we "defend" in our egos.) Since I didn't catch what she said the first time, I waited until after she hung up and listened as my *secondary hearing* (from Spirit) kicked in and I heard Jo say, "You are *not* my friend! I don't want you to ever write or call me again!" Her receiver was slammed down, and I could *feel* it 2700 miles away. (Since nothing occurs in our life that is *not* our wish, or state of consciousness to include fear and guilt for the past, Jo's fears or guilt called the message in my letter into her life. It was an *answer to her prayer* to forgive her father, once and for all.)

Well, that may have been the end of Jay and Jo's physical relationship, but not *my* spiritual relationship with her. A friend recently remarked how well I was taking Jo's and my potentially permanent separation. I told her that was because it was my "love" for her *Spirit* (essence) that mattered, not her body, and that can never be changed by anyone and will *always* be! You have to "completely" love/forgive your self (or be approaching it) *first* to get to that recognition point. I also told this friend that if I had to do it over again, I still would have mailed the letter that ended our relationship. To help a friend look at their ego (when they are *able* or *supposed to*) and go *beyond* all fear, is worth more than any "physical" relationship!

I did see Josephine one time, three weeks after I landed back in Florida to help my mother out shortly after my dad died on the fourth of July. (I tried to *see* her as soon as I arrived at 10:15 P.M....I even brought a rose and a written apology for being the "vehicle" of the infamous letter, but she wouldn't open the door or talk with me.) I had stopped at her apartment just before she was going out on a dinner date and *tried* to explain how the letter came to be and about the fact that when she told me of her not being able to forgive her father totally that I became her "answer to prayer" (meaning the vehicle for her *call for help* so that she could see her similarities with him, and therefore, forgive *herself* "in" him). It didn't seem to register because she told me that she had gone on her with her life, so I looked into her eyes and said, "I've *always* 'really' loved you from when we first met." I gave her a hug and left.

I guess the most important lesson I learned from this was *not seeing* "human" error in someone *from our ego* because to do so makes it real. I paid a big price to learn this! We all are responsible for *how* we see another (either extending love or calling for it), because our perception of them is "our" *mis*creation of them (we are formless, eternal Spirit in reality). I have since learned that we can only *love* someone *unconditionally* without "any" correction, unless asked for by them (as I "felt" that Jo had...indirectly), to let our Truthful-*consciousness* and presence support them in being "open" about themselves *with* themselves.

*   *   *

There are two other anecdotes about Jo and me that are cute and meaningful to us on the psychic-level of the physical (*ego*) world. A "spiritualist" minister (who deals in mediumship rather than *real* Spirit) was staying for a week at the same house I was living in, over two years ago. I was sitting in the living room reading when he walked up to me after his fourth and last evening seminar and said, "This is an *aport*. It is from the *other* (*s*pirit) world. Your soul-mate has the duplicate." He then folded my fingers over what appeared to be a shiny, pink crystal that he put in the palm of my hand. Because I am *primarily* interested in the "internal awareness" of God/Spirit (the consciousness of a mystic), I care *nothing* about the psychic realm of the *worldly*, separate-identity oriented "ego," and never asked him anything about "psychic-stuff" during the several days we lived together under the same roof. He was a very nice, gentle soul. I put it in my pocket, thought it would be nice to have a "spiritual partner" and forgot about it, until a year later I found the *match* to it sitting on Jo's dresser. She silently, but visibly, "freaked out" when I showed them to her.

The next "sign" we had of our soul-connection was the day we walked out to my car, and I pulled down a 5" x 6" copy of my favorite picture from above the visor on the passenger side. It was of Sallman's painting, Good Shepherd, of Jesus amongst a flock of sheep beside a stream in a mountain canyon holding a baby lamb in his arms. Jo stood up real straight and said, "Oh, my God!" (She had pasted the *same* picture, but a much larger copy, on the *same color* green, cardboard mat as the border on my copy.) "I guess we're supposed to be soul-mates," I said. She agreed, in disbelief, or should I say, *shock*.

*   *   *

Jo was, and still is, *the* greatest inspiration in my life...or put more accurately, in Truth, *my* love for her **essence** is. I *loved* the Spirit in her (represented on Earth by the heart-felt mind, *not* the brain), and my "human ego" *liked* her form very much. But, her body was *not* the focus of my relationship with her, which is what I thought *every* woman wanted (as they usually say, "I want you to love me for my mind, not my body!"...although Jo's ego once stated that *it* wanted the reverse, if you can imagine that). That's why I only missed her *physical* presence when I left for Utah.

During our first two short separations, I completed two books of poetry in *two days* that I had started *seven years prior* to meeting her. In December, while we were together, I completed a short novel about our mind-explorations in search of learning how to just "be" on Earth while knowing the Truth about it's "dream-like" quality (something I had been struggling with, also for *seven years*). I felt so frustrated by my inability to communicate with Jo, in any way, at the *end* of our physical relationship that I felt compelled to write another novelistic-type book about spiritual (?) relationships (realizing that in "wholly"/holy relationships people do *not* "need" each other) and *why* they fail (?) or end.

After *five* spiritual partnerships and the loss of the "female version of Jay" (Jo's words), I was determined to at least have a sense of completion and understanding to *heal my self*, my partners and, perhaps, the entire universe...since *everything* we do consciously contributes to it. What a terrible thing it is to go deep into Spirit (Peacefulness and Contentment) with someone, only to have them fall back into the ego-world and walk or run away. (Since *most* of Jo's and my time together was spent in a meditative consciousness, I considered it almost monastic in its depth.) Jo's departure caused me anguish for so long...IT was the last straw!

Perhaps, when I left last February, Jo remembered her traumatic past loss of a deep love relationship, which scared her (ego) into believing (without considering her *own* obvious lack of commitment to our relationship) that I was gone for good (once again, after Australia)..."leavers" can't stand *being left*, so they leave *first*!...me, too! Since they feel guilty for their insecurity (which ultimately comes from the "belief," that *everyone* on Earth suffers from, that God is going to punish them for *leaving heaven*, the state of One-consciousness, to be "special" in this *dream* world that we *THINK* we live in), their ego's get caught up in finding fault with and blaming their lover for his or her ego characteristics. She feared being left alone, like me, so she "substituted" (found) another lover (as *all* the others had). Oh, these mirrors?!...these "dream *projections*" of *our* self onto another form.

Josephine's humanness has a quality I have only clearly seen before in Roseanne (after she was gone) that is as an "adaptive" whereby *it* becomes like the personality of the closest friend, associate or hero/idol that it has. Two months after I left Florida, Jo's ego became like her "flaky" female friend that she was hanging around with. (Yes, Jo could have taken on *my* characteristics while in my physical proximity or consciousness, which is very possible. And no, I would not want her, or anyone, to imitate me unless they *truly believed* in their heart what I believe. Since Jo and I believed in absolute Truth, it would be appropriate for her to demonstrate traits of peacefulness and contentment like mine. And, I have no doubt that I served as a *reminder* of that consciousness for her, as I hopefully do for everyone, and that she *acted* like me. Ideally, we all learn to develop a peaceful, loving demeanor that is our *own*, and cannot be affected by others who come into our life.)

*   *   *

A psychic friend mentioned that because Jo was joined with me on the mind-level that her ego may have become frightened of becoming a mental "yes-man" to me (I certainly hoped not, but it was a reasonable possibility...I would not want a "robot" for a spiritual partner and lover, so I hoped my friend was wrong.) I knew that Jo resented "authority figures" (yet she became one at home and work) and pretentious, "titled" people like CPA's (but she wanted to be known by the *old-fashioned* title of <u>Comp</u>troller). She hated *any* criticism...the slightest innuendo about her character (ego) would send *it* into a "tail-spin" (must be the Irish in it. A mirror of my super-sensitive and withdrawn past). Since Jo was a Controller (making good money as the number two person of her company...people who "become" their position and the money associated with it are *very* insecure) and had a former husband who didn't want to work, I think "being taken care of" was an *unrecognized* concern of hers, particularly since her father "quit" his 25 year career in the military *without* a pension (but, she was *very* generous).

When I first started going out with Jo, she seemed to be highly nervous, sometimes to the point that she would "shake" or twitch all over, which she attributed to

-82-

a physical quality of her mother's (she inherited it, in other words). I told her that she didn't have to do it anymore (I sounded like a "psychic" in that moment) and that it was just a general fearfulness that caused it. She hardly ever shook or appeared nervous again after that. (The power of others' suggestions could have a strong effect on Jo...if, she believed in them.)

But, I think Jo's *major* fear, as was mine, was of making a 100% complete commitment to another person in a relationship. The possibility of surrendering completely to another causes our egos to scramble to do anything to kill the relationship. I had heard that when I had been gone awhile Jo's ego (not the *real* person I loved) found a lot of fault with me...particularly *after* I sent the infamous letter that exposed her ego's major faults ("monkey see...monkey do!").

*   *   *

In addition to feeling scared by Jo's preoccupation with her job, I found out a very important lesson in Salt Lake City...that it was no longer my "home" and that no *place* was. That was terribly unsettling to me...to the point that I wondered what I was doing here on Earth. I was *afraid* when I first got there that if I talked with Jo on the telephone and she told me she missed me that I would have turned right around and come back to Florida to her...and, I knew, in my mind, that I could only finish my four books there. Such a quandary!

My biggest ego fear was the thought of being alone

forever without anyone to give love to who could under-stand and *live* absolute Truth to the degree I did. (I know a lot of people who understand it, intellectually, but still *live* their life like an "earthling," mentally.) While I was in Salt Lake, I felt emotionally *comatose* (like I had no feelings at all) and that I was all alone in this world, spiritually. It wasn't until I arrived back in Florida five months later, to help my mother out and to attend my oldest daughter's wedding, that I began to "feel" again. When I tried to get in touch with Josephine, she blocked my efforts, and *then* I started to feel helpless and fearful (which is better than *no* feelings). I hate to say it, but I guess I had to lose someone very important to me to break through my "ego" *encased in denial (repression)* and devoid of feelings to bring them up. "Withdrawal" was my human way of being over-sensitive and over-reactive by avoiding emotional confrontation with my fear of dealing with others' anger or rage like Jo's, which was *her* way of being over-sensitive and over-reactive. (Like attracts like...but, the manifestation can take a different form!)

*   *   *

I came to bring "clarity" into Jo's life about the Truth (she didn't *realize* that God did not make the Earth, even though she had read it) as was evidenced by the new glasses I bought her, which she needed badly. I brought her flowers for the first time in her life, at 44. I also demonstrated my spiritual commitment to our brother-hood by focusing on her mind rather than her body.

One time when we had gone to the beach, Jo fainted while we were leaving. I kneeled over her to shield her from the sun until she came to. I remember thinking (listening) while I was looking at her innocence all crumpled in the sand, "It's okay if you want to leave Earth now." In that instant, I realized that I *truly* loved her...because, I was "willing" to give her the *freedom* to go, forever!

★　　　　　★　　　　　★

Together, at the *same exact time*, we discovered that we shared the *identical*, real "life purpose" of *bringing love* to the world...although she saw herself as an object (love bringer); and I, as a function (to bring love)...when we attended a spiritual retreat. We had the greatest freedom in our relationship as evidenced by the fact that we had been able to totally release in mutual (my first), multi-orgasmic experiences.

★　　　　　★　　　　　★

Jo was the *most* wonderfully "beautiful," sexy, adorable, unconditionally loving, kind, generous, innocent and mystical/spiritual woman of my life, who learned the hardest lesson to *accept* about the unreality of the dream-world we live (die) in. She also rose above a major sexual-block *instantly* on the human level, which many people would have taken a lifetime to get over...if ever. She was the most tender, gentle and sincere blessing I have ever known...a true angel!

The Innocence

I saw
their innocence
as a
child-like being,
which drew
me near.
(Little did
I know
that it was
my own.)

Epilogue
(Puppy Dog Man and
the Cat Women)

When I was a teenager, my mother said, "You were never happy unless you had a girl-friend." That was because I came from a family environment where *I* felt "totally" unappreciated, unloved and unsupported, and being an individual that needed a lot of love (and the *only* way we "receive" love is when we *give* it), I found great happiness in having someone in my life to give love to and who appreciated the *essence* in me that gave it. By today's standards, I probably would have been considered a dependent person if my happiness was contingent upon making someonelse feel loved...actually, I learned recently that it is *not* unusual or unnatural, *spiritually*, to love another *as your Self.*

There is a *very* fine line between love and "need." The difference is that if you love your self (and *I AM* my own best friend, critic and support system), it is perfectly natural to *express* (give) love to others in the *dream*...which may involve nothing more than just *being* with them regardless of what their "ego" may want or think it needs.

Another thing that has become important for me, and us, to remember is that the mind is "split" (we are all schizophrenic!)...meaning that we vacillate back and forth between the *human* ego and the Spirit-guided, "right-minded" ego, constantly...and, whenever we are in *any* kind of pain or discomfort or defensiveness, we need to "grow up" and LOOK AT our selves to see what consciousness we are coming from and *change it* and our attitude. (No one can live on Earth without an ego...a "belief" in themselves as a human being. When we rise *totally* beyond it, then we are no longer in "form.")

Personally, I think it's wonderful to have someone special to care and do things for, and I can't think of one thing that can "humanly" top it. I am aware, from time to time, of what it's like to be in a *real* spiritual consciousness with Love/God/the Universe, which *far exceeds* the "human" experience. If I had my ego preference, I'd be just like a little puppy dog (as I have acted in the past) with the woman of my *human* choosing...although I know now that we attract "spiritual learning lessons" as well. (I've noticed in *my* world, looking back over the past, that women *generally* act like distrustful and cautious "cats;" whereas, men *tend* to play loyal companions who fall at their feet willing to do their bidding at the slightest provocation like "puppy dogs"...in <u>loving</u> relationships.) I hope to graduate to total self-less Love at some point, but I do enjoy some real good, Spirit-filled human company at "home" *wherever* I am.

Since *everyone* on Earth feels guilt for separating themself from God (the ultimate fear) to live in a limited, physical form, and very few are probably *aware* of that consciousness even though they understand it intellectually, we *all* don't feel *truly* "worthy" of being loved! What I have discovered through this is that I *unconsciously* have attracted into my life women who feel the *same* way as I and who *unconsciously* are "helping" me (my ego) to fulfill my "wish/fear" (remember a "fear" is a *thought* which has the same effect as a "wish") of my unworthiness by *rejecting* me and running away (their demonstration of their unworthiness) from our relationship. Since all minds are joined, particularly those with whom we have a close, love relationship, our lovers help us to play out our wishes, which include things we don't even realize about ourself, consciously. (There are no *victims*...only "volunteers"!) "So, thank you ladies for showing me how to forgive myself by holding up the mirror of *my* fears (remember the *specific* manifestation isn't important...just the presence of fear in others that causes a *reaction* in us is)! Bless you...all!"

A final realization came to me when I was through looking at my self in all my past love relationships. I noticed that I had a very subtle, *suppressed* "anger" that began with the birth process whereby I (and we) had my (our) first encounter with *separation/rejection* from my (our) mother, who represented the Universe at that point...which is the root cause (symptom) of my (our) *sense of unworthiness*. My separations (rejections) in my relationships were nothing more than <u>reenactments</u> of the *initial* separation at birth (which symbolizes our departure from Spirit/God) until I caught on to this and forgave my **ego-self** for creating these situations out of fear and guilt for leaving my heavenly consciousness, and formlessness. Once I REALIZED that my human self was "angry" about losing people in my life and would try *tenaciously* to retrieve them, its game was over! The *human* ego is like a little child (regardless of how old we are), and it will try to get its own way, which means holding onto people and aspects of the *dream* that it likes. The task at hand now becomes to learn to wait patiently until the "worthy" people, who feel good about themselves, walk into my life...but, the lessons may continue!

      *   *   *

"Well, Ralphy"...who was still lying with his eyes closed in the hammock..."I hope I haven't put you to sleep with all this?"

"No, of course not!" as he opened his eyes. "I was glad you really dug into it. That's the only way we *really* get FREE. Were you aware of many of these insights while you were *in* them?"

"Yes, to a limited degree. Beginning with Roseanne, I was very much aware of my spiritual brotherhood with each of them. As a matter of fact, that was my *primary* focus from the beginning, plus, my humanness found them very 'attractive'...not so much in terms of physical beauty, but they all had this 'innocence' (particularly Jo, who was mesmerizing), this child-like Christ-being, that pulled me to them. Actually, I later learned that "it takes one to know one" (*the* most important *spiritual* lesson) and that it was my *own* innocence or spiritual essence that I was seeing in them.

"I also learned to *accept* that I drew them to me because I was *willing* and ready to look at *my* ego characteristics and fears *in* them. Suzanne was my mirror of my financial insecurity and self-concern (ego-centeredness); Roseanne was my fear of losing my independence; Sandy, my fear of being abandoned; Connie was my fear of not belonging or fitting in; Robilee was my fear of losing control of my life; and Josephine held up the mirror of my fear of not being taken care of and not being appreciated as well as being the manifestation of *every* significant woman of my past...which was kind of wild! And...they *all* showed me *my* 'finickiness.'

"I know now that if *any* ego quality in another person causes me even the *slightest* discomfort or negative value judgment about them I have not forgiven that aspect of *my* ego's past. Remember, Ralphy, this world is just a <u>waking dream</u>, and that as *aspects* of the *one* Son of God, who is sleeping dreaming of us, our lesson is to *realize* that and to not take life too seriously...we *are* supposed to uncover our fears and ego attributes though! That's why I had you here...to be a sounding board to help me dig up all my relationship-stuff."

"Since it has helped me to see some things in myself,

too, Jay-Jay, I appreciate the opportunity...as always...to help. Afterall, as I learned from you, <u>WE'RE JUST HERE TO DISCOVER 'WHAT' (Spirit) WE ARE AND TO BE A FRIEND TO OTHERS COMING ALONG THE ROAD 'HOME.'</u> That's what 'real' relationships are all about!"

"You know, since I began this introspection (which I am famous for according to my close friends), I kept asking, 'Why am I searching for answers about a *dream* if I'm a *developing* mystic and am more concerned with learning to turn *inward* <u>all</u> the time and to *unfocus* on the physical world and people's egos? Why does anything happen in a dream...because *it's a dream*!!' Then I got my answer: 'Because *I* want *more* company!'

I sat up straight and started gliding the porch swing back and forth more rapidly, now. "I wanted to find the answers, on the earth-level we live on, that will help others to look at themselves to go *beyond* their human selves. If *I* won't do it and show how it's done, how can *I* expect my family and friends to? Teaching is *demonstration*! You know that!"

"Yep. You repeated it many, many times so that I wouldn't forget," said Ralph, who sat up and threw his legs over the edge of the hammock and let them dangle, barely touching the ground.

We both sat and stared out over the sandy knoll and the tall cedar trees and listened to the silence. It was wonderful. Funny how peacefulness can become such a great, pleasurable pastime. I love it more than anything. That's why a quiet walk is such a peaceful meditation...like being with the entire "Love" of the universe...my higher Self.

I continued, "That's why I want to put all this in a book, because if I can *share* it with as many people as possible so they can arrive at the same awareness of Spirit, I'll have more company. Pretty selfish, huh...to want more company on the human level? Since *we* are here consciously on the physical plane most of the time, we have to *train* our egos to be more disciplined (or right-minded) in keeping AWARE of our purpose to wake-up and *feel* the 'Love' that we are, with *no* thoughts or feelings of hate, anger or fear."

"I guess when *we* realize that is ALL we have to do, Jay-Jay, we will wake-up. But, until people see that and feel justified in their separate ego-minds that they have had *enough* pain and it's worth doing, they won't."

"You're right. But *everyone* reaches a saturation point, as I did when I was 38, and again at 45, where nothing and no one *of* the 'physical' world can satisfy them anymore. That's why I wrote *BANISHED...From The Sandbox*...to share with as many people as possible what happens *inside*, as it did in my life, when we get to that point so *they* hopefully wouldn't feel strange or weird, know they are not alone and not do anything inappropriate (like taking their own life) *before* they reached a 'state of mind' of *total forgiveness* and peace. Since *all* death is suicide because no one comes into this dream-world to 'live,' I will not *value* judge one person's form of leaving the dream over another's *more accept-*

able (but perhaps, less honest) way of departing, like through some painful illness such as cancer or a heart attack."

"And your purpose in this book is going to be...?" asked Ralph.

"To discover what *I* need to learn to forgive in myself that is held up in the mirrors of my five spiritual partners since that is *why* we all come to Earth, in *spiritual* terms (the ego came to 'play' and avoid our reality). Without looking at what in ME caused the end of our relationships, I will *never* be able to live in peaceful contentment (my *realization* of 'total' happiness). Also, I hope that it might benefit their own self-examination. I figure that if I want *real, spiritual* people and *a* spiritual partner in my dream, I'd better be the most excellent example of what I want. I'm committed to it!"

"Well, you're doing all right, kid!"

"Thanks, Ralphy! Coming from you, that's a *real* compliment."

"Have you come to any conclusions from all this?" asked Ralph.

"Yes. First of all, I came to understand that all five of my spiritual partners showed me *one* major fault of mine. What I saw in *all* of them was *my* inability to make a *100%* commitment to a relationship (because anything less is *not* a commitment). I realized, as they demonstrated, that by not letting go of my 'self-concern' about *losing control* or the *fear of being controlled* I would not attain it.

"We are all 'afraid' of *Love* more than anythingelse because we don't believe (unconsciously) we are *worthy* of it because we separated ourselves (we think) from God. When I've come to the point in a relationship where I have to surrender my ego's desires to be willing to just love another and make them *equally* important as my-self, my human ego rears up and says, 'Run away...you don't need this person and their *problems* (learning lessons) to make your life difficult...you deserve to have a comfortable, easy life.' Unfortunately, we don't learn to go beyond fear by avoiding conflict as I have done...we have to learn to be peaceful in chaotic situations and to see them as a 'call for love.'

"Since my biggest fear is *being abandoned*, the women in my life have *cooperated with me* (my ego) on the mind-level to give me what I *felt* worthy of...no love...and ran away.

"Secondly, if they did not *truly* 'love' themselves, as I have not (again, my mirror), by forgiving their past fears and guilt that they projected onto me *through anger*, how could I expect them to love me? You can only have a 'complete' and *real* relationship with someone who truly recognizes (loves) themselves *beyond* their human-ness and is not tied to (dependent upon) *any* body-stuff. (Quite frankly, I don't know if it's possible on Earth!)"

"That makes sense," interjected Ralph.

"Next, I discovered that our minds can become so

totally joined, as mine and Jo's did, that the *slightest* displeasure (mentally) on *my* part with her ego could be felt by *her* mind (actually, there is only *one* mind, and we both tapped into it) and responded to by her running away. For instance, very early one morning Jo got up and *bolted* out of bed as soon as she awoke, got dressed, said something incoherent about ending our relationship and left my house. We had not had *any* argument, disagreement or fight (practically ever) the night before (we went to bed peacefully and had made love gently). My inner voice told me that Jo left in anger because she had 'mentally' picked up, as she had done *so often* before being a 'sensitive' (psychic), that I did not want *only* her anymore (I met an attractive woman the evening before that I wanted to socialize with or pursue). Very scary...when you realize that your thoughts are *not* your *own* anymore. Jo gave me the *freedom* (which is 'what' love is) to go after this other woman by leaving me! (When she left me the fourth and final time, I did not give her the same freedom, I held on like *crazy*...literally!)

"People have 'no idea' how powerful the mind is and how connected (adaptive) we *all* are, and particularly *spiritual partners* since that is the *primary* basis of their relationship. Being loving is their function by being *peaceful at all times*, but if either partner lets their ego takeover, as Jo did for instance when she went into a rage at the end of our relationship, the physical aspect of it ends...unless, that individual regroups and takes control of their ego-emotions to get peaceful rather than avoiding dealing with it by seeking *other* social, sexual or occupational associations to occupy their ego-mind. (The mind can be trained, by 'willingness,' to surrender control of one's ego-life; thereby allowing the mind to *listen* to its internal guidance from the Peaceful Heart, which is the *way of the mystic*...not psychic.)

"Finally, I agree with my friend, Richard, who said, 'The *only* thing of importance here on Earth is the *quality of our loving.*' To live in peace and learn to unconditionally love *all* people by overlooking and not commenting on (*value* judging) their human-ego games, and characteristics, is my *only* goal and contribution to attaining that quality. I feel I have walked alone long enough now, and I choose to walk *primarily* with like-minded, aware, loving, gentle mystical people...but, not avoid the others.

"My female spiritual partner will also be of like mind as myself as I do not want to have to train or teach her anything about absolute Truth. I do *not* want to be her idol or mentor (there is nothing wrong with appreciation and respect, though). If I am going to *be* 'whole,' then I no longer can *play* rescuer/rescuee (yes, if I play one, then I am the *other*, because of my neediness to be 'needed')! I *played* 'mentor' to all my past spiritual partners to give them love in the form of knowledge of the Truth, and they gave me idol-worship/love (?) that I thought I *needed* to 'rescue' myself from *my* own victimization of my *ego*-created poor self-esteem from 'being' in my *human* consciousness. (They actually became my teachers while I taught *my* human self, which is all anyone teaches, how to understand Truth in depth...it's all *ego*-training, in other words, since this is where we are.)

"No more 'spiritual plebeians' who are not *committed* to gently 'walk-the-walk'...anyone's ego can 'talk-the-talk.' Maybe the mystical walk home is a *separate* and singular journey since everything takes place in our *own* mind. But, that does not preclude us from walking together in mutual respect and acceptance of our brotherhood. As Teri said so succinctly, 'Love is *not* the reason for relationship; common purpose is.' Hopefully, *our* purpose is *to love* by 'forgiving/overlooking' our humanness that we see in others.

"*Maybe* I also came into my spiritual partners' lives under the guise of 'romantic love' to bring them a touch of *unconditional* love from our Father...to let them know that they are *always* loved no matter how they act or if they run away to play again in the 'sandbox' called the world. All of them did thank me for that.

"Until we accept *complete* responsibility, and *I* do, for bringing the people that we do into our lives and learning *our* lessons about *ourselves* from them, we cannot make a *real* commitment to take care of anyonelse."

"AMEN!" said Ralph as he stood up and clapped.

I jokingly, with a big childish grin on my face, stopped swinging, stood up and facing left toward Ralph, bowed at the waist.

*   *   *

I won't forget this experience and the lessons it taught me about wanting to put someonelse first *before* (but not sacrificing) myself; not becoming devoid of feelings (mentally running away) when approached with tension-riddled, fearful relationship encounters; not avoiding difficult relationship encounters; and that only commitment of *both* parties in a relationship to *living* the Truth can keep it peaceful and together *physically* on Earth. Most of all, I learned that I have to LET GO of someone when they want to leave...no matter what the reason! I forgive my self and my "soul-mates" for failing to communicate *all* of our feelings and fears openly and for running away. (Yes, "developing" mystics have work to do on this earthly level, too! No *body* is perfect on Earth; otherwise, they wouldn't be here.)

Mystics walk through the "fire" of their own fear by *looking* at *all* of it! And...they don't look for "soul" (an attempt to attribute Spirit *with* the body) in another person! *Everyone* is your "spiritual" partner!

EPITAPH
FOR THE EARTHBOUND

WHEN WE "OWN" WHAT WE SEE IN THE *MIRROR*, IT AND WE WILL CHANGE FOR THE BETTER. PEOPLE WHO CAN <u>NOT</u> EXPOSE THEIR FEARS AND EGO-TRAITS TO THEMSELVES ARE *TRAPPED* IN THE "HELL" OF THEIR OWN MINDS UNTIL THEY DO!

(*ACKNOWLEDGMENT* IS THE KEY TO RELEASE AND FREEDOM.)

this is the <u>ONLY</u> lesson:

"THIS IS BUT A DREAM!"

(There are *no* answers! But... you will not realize this until you have *awakened* and can see the "dream" while you are *in* it from a place in your mind *beyond* it. *Some* form of "peace" is your answer!)

The Lesson

Everything here
is as I see it.
It is not *Truth,*
universally.
It's...
"individual" perception,
which is all
any of us
have.
If I "react
to anything,
that is what
I have to
work on next.